Concurrences Books

Tributes

Eleanor Fox – Liber Amicorum
Nicolas Charbit et al. (eds.), 2021

Herbert Hovenkamp – The Dean of American Antitrust Law
Nicolas Charbit et al. (eds.), 2021

Albert Foer – A Consumer Voice in the Antitrust Arena
Nicolas Charbit et al. (eds.), 2020

Richard Whish – Taking Competition Law Outside the Box
Nicolas Charbit et al. (eds.), 2020

Frédéric Jenny – Standing Up for Convergence and Relevance in Antitrust, Vol. I & II
Nicolas Charbit et al. (eds.), 2019 & 2021

Wang Xiaoye – The Pioneer of Competition Law in China
Adrian Emch, Wendy Ng (ed.), 2019

Douglas H. Ginsburg – An Antitrust Professor on the Bench, Vol. I & II
Nicolas Charbit et al. (eds.), 2018 & 2020

Ian S. Forrester – A Scot Without Borders, Vol. I & II
Assimakis Komninos et al. (ed.), 2015

William E. Kovacic – An Antitrust Tribute, Vol. I & II
Nicolas Charbit et al. (eds.), 2013 & 2014

Practical Books

Global Dictionary of Competition Law
Deborah Healey, William Kovacic, Pablo Trevisan, Richard Whish (eds.), 2022

State Aid & National Enforcement
Jacques Derenne, Denis Jouve, Christophe Lemaire, Francesco Martucci (eds.), 2022

Perspectives on Antitrust Compliance
Anne Riley, Andreas Stephan, Anny Tubbs (eds.), 2021

Information Exchange and Related Risks – A Practical Guide
Marcio Dias Soares (ed.), 2021

Merger Control in Latin America – A Jurisdictional Guide
Paulo Burnier da Silveira & Pamela Sittenfeld (eds.), 2020

Competition Inspections under EU Law
Nathalie Jalabert-Doury, 2020

Competition Digest – A Synthesis of EU, US and National Leading Cases, 4th ed.
Frédéric Jenny (ed.), 2020

Gun Jumping in Merger Control – A Jurisdictional Guide
Catriona Hatton, Yves Comtois, Andrea Hamilton (eds.), 2019

Choice – A New Standard for Competition Analysis?
Paul Nihoul et al., 2016

PhD Theses

The Role of Media Pluralism in the Enforcement of EU Competition Law
Konstantina Bania, 2019

Buyer Power in EU Competition Law
Ignacio Herrera Anchustegui, 2017

General Interest

Women & Antitrust – Voices from the Field, Vol. I & II
Evelina Kurgonaite & Kristina Nordlander (eds.), 2020

Conference Proceedings

Antitrust in Emerging and Developing Countries, Vol I & II
Eleanor Fox, Harry First (eds.), 2015 & 2016

Global Antitrust Law – Current Issues in Antitrust Law and Economics
Douglas Ginsburg, Joshua Wright (eds.), 2015

Competition Law on the Global Stage: David Gerber's Global Competition Law in Perspective
David Gerber, 2014

e-Book versions available for **Concurrences+** subscribers

Competition and Regulation in Network Industries

Essays in Industrial Organisation

Jean-Marc Zogheib

Foreword by Marc Bourreau
Introduction by Frédéric Marty

Concurrences, 2021

PhD Award Concurrences

106 West 32nd Street, Suite 144 New York, NY, 10001, USA
www.concurrences.com
book@concurrences.com

First Printing, October 2021
978-1-954750-99-9 (Paperback)
Library of Congress Control Number: 2021918622

Cover Design: Yves Buliard, www.yvesbuliard.fr
Book Design and Layout implementation: Nord Compo

INSTITUT POLYTECHNIQUE DE PARIS

Competition and Regulation in Network Industries

Essays in Industrial Organisation

THÈSE DE DOCTORAT DE L'INSTITUT POLYTECHNIQUE DE PARIS

Préparée à Telecom Paris

École doctorale n° 626 de l'Institut Polytechnique de Paris (IPP)

Spécialité de doctorat : Sciences Economiques

Thèse présentée et soutenue à Paris, le 11 Octobre 2019, par

Jean-Marc ZOGHEIB

Composition du Jury

Maya BACACHE
Professeur, Telecom Paris (Présidente)

Axel GAUTIER
Professeur, HEC Management School-ULG (Rapporteur)

Edmond BARANÈS
Professeur, Université de Montpellier (Rapporteur)

Wilfried SAND-ZANTMAN
Professeur, ESSEC Business School (Examinateur)

François JEANJEAN
Ingénieur de recherche, Orange (Examinateur)

Marc BOURREAU
Professeur, Telecom Paris (Directeur de thèse)

DISCLAIMER

This book is based on a doctoral thesis defended in 2019 at the Institut Polytechnique de Paris (Telecom Paris) before a jury composed of Ms. Maya Bacache (Professor at Telecom Paris), Mr. Marc Bourreau (Professor at Telecom Paris), Mr. Axel Gautier (Professor at HEC Management School – ULG), Mr. Edmond Baranès (Professor at the University of Montpellier), Mr. Wilfried Sand-Zantman (Professor at the ESSEC Business School), and Mr. François Jeanjean (Research Engineer at Orange).

The book has been slightly modified so that its "scientific apparatus" is as up-to-date as possible.

The author declares that there is no conflict of interest associated with this publication. The opinions expressed in this book are those of the author. Telecom Paris (Institut Polytechnique de Paris) neither approves nor disapproves of them. The book won the Concurrences PhD Award in Economics 2020, chaired by Professor Frédéric Marty (CNRS) and composed of Philippe Février (CREST & Veltys), Emmanuel Frot (Analysis Group), Tommaso Valletti (Imperial College London), and Hal Varian (Google).

Table of Contents

INTRODUCTION

It was a great honour for me to chair the first jury established by the journal Concurrences to award a thesis prize in economics.

This prize is now taking its place alongside the one awarded for many years in law and, in my opinion, testifies to the transdisciplinarity intrinsic to our field. In the same way that legal doctrine feeds on decision-making practice and fertilises it in return, economics is even more accurate in terms of understanding market strategies and effective in terms of public policy recommendations and of legal frameworks evolutions' proposals when it resolutely engages in a dual dialogue with legal sciences and the practice of jurisdictions.

This legal economic-nexus was at the heart of the approach of the American institutionalist economists who in the 1920s coined the term law and economics. Such an approach at the confluence of economics, law and competition practice is not the prerogative of law and economics alone. This is naturally also true for the Concurrences prize. It is intended to cover a broad disciplinary spectrum from political economy to industrial economics.

This is the framework for the thesis of Jean-Marc Zogheib, who was the winner of our first prize and of this first publication. Beyond its exceptional formal qualities and the rigour of its approach, which readers will discover upon reading this work, a few points seem essential to me. This work covers – through the modelling tools used in IO – a particularly representative field of the possible contributions of economic analysis to competition and regulatory law issues.

One of the major interests of Jean-Marc Zogheib's work is to show the extent to which regulatory and competition policies are intertwined and must be considered as complementary rather than substitutable instruments. The current debates on the Digital Markets Act show the need to reconsider this link between ex ante and ex post interventions, which is a key factor not only for the distribution of tasks between the various public policies but also for the enforcement of competition policies, which by their very nature play on both dimensions.

This articulation between ex ante and ex post is one of the structuring lines of this book in each of the three essays that structure it and which, as we have noted, cover a wide spectrum of competition issues. The first essay deals with merger control, the second with the framework for state aid and the third with the integration of possible exploitative practices related to data in the implementation of mergers' control in digital markets.

The first contribution deals with merger control. It highlights the impact of control on firms' strategies by showing how they internalise the constraints in their decision-making. The model developed by Jean-Marc Zogheib is based on a trade-off between a merger-acquisition project in the same regional area or in a territory located elsewhere. He shows that the relative rigour of merger control may lead firms to favour the second type of project despite lower efficiency gains.

The second contribution shifts the focus to the area of state aid regulation by considering investments in network infrastructure. Once again, the connections with the major issues related to the reconciliation between firms' strategies and competition policy are at the heart of the analysis. It is not a question here of reconciling industrial policy and competition policy as in the first essay. It is a question here of reconciling competition (and sectoral liberalisation) with the assumption of responsibility for regional development policies and therefore for territorial economic attractiveness. The case in hand is that of the complementarity of public and private investment in the deployment of very high-speed telecommunications infrastructures. The parallel with the deployment plans implemented at national and EU level shows the interest of economic reflection on the subject. Public intervention must be adjusted and proportionate to correct market failure.

The third essay sheds light on another decisive dimension of current competitive issues, which is the functioning of digital markets and the regulation of the practices of dominant firms with regard to both their commercial partners and consumers. These anti-competitive practices include exploitative practices that do not result in overpricing but in excessive data extraction. The damage to the consumer takes the form of damage to privacy, the effects of which will depend on whether or not the consumer is on one or more platforms (i.e. whether he or she chooses to opt for single or multi-homing). This last chapter considers the impacts of mergers not only from the point of view of their impact on prices but also from the point of view of the protection of privacy as a function of consumers' choice between single and multi-homing.

It is therefore a tour de force that Jean-Marc Zogheib has succeeded in achieving in his thesis such an overview of everything that IO can contribute to the competition law related issues. The quality of this work lies in this precious combination of rigorous economic analysis and openness to current competitive and regulatory issues. His work shows that economics can contribute some essential building blocks to the construction of competitive reasoning and symmetrically that the integration of competition law into economic models contributes to extending their scope and collective usefulness.

Frédéric MARTY
Research Fellow, Centre National de la Recherche Scientifique (CNRS)
Board Member, French Competition Authority

FOREWORD

It is with great pleasure that I write the preface to this book by Mr. Jean-Marc Zogheib, which results from the doctoral research that I had the honour of supervising. This publication represents a significant achievement of research done with great talent on innovative and policy relevant subjects.

In his research, Mr. Zogheib focuses on network industries, such as telecommunications or the digital sector. Network industries are particularly dynamic and innovative and represent an essential source of growth for our economies. Network industries are characterised by economies of scale and scope in the production of products and services, and network effects in the consumption of goods, generating increasing returns for firms. Increasing returns imply a strong tendency towards concentration, with the emergence of natural monopolies in extreme cases. As a result, firms in network industries may acquire strong market power, raising concerns from competition and regulatory authorities. The general objective of Mr. Zogheib's research is to study the interplay between public policy and firms' strategies in network industries. How do firms react to the rules set by public policy? If their strategic reaction is accounted for, are the objectives of public intervention still being achieved?

A great strength of Mr. Zogheib's research is that he combines various tools of theoretical economic analysis – adopted from industrial economics, network economics and platform economics – to shed light on highly topical issues in the telecommunications and digital sectors.

Mr. Zogheib's thesis consists of three distinct parts, each focused on a specific research topic.

In the first chapter of his thesis, Mr. Zogheib examines how merger control can affect a firm's choice between a local, in-market merger and a cross-border merger. Mr. Zogheib argues that cross-border mergers represent a higher level of risk for firms than in-market mergers. For example, a firm may imperfectly anticipate the organisational difficulties of a cross-border merger due to a lack of relevant information on the foreign market. If the cross-border merger fails, the merging firm may exit the foreign market by selling its foreign subsidiary to a local player, leading to a merger in that market. However, if the merger control policy is particularly strict, the outcome of this local merger may be uncertain. In that case, the firm faces a barrier to exit (by merger), and from an ex-ante perspective, a barrier to entry through cross-border mergers. In this work, Mr. Zogheib highlights that merger policy may affect firms' entry strategies – whether they are local or cross-border – by raising barriers to exit by merger.

In the second chapter, Mr. Zogheib focuses on the role of public players in the deployment of new network infrastructures, such as fibre access networks. The very high rollout costs of network technologies have pushed public players to invest alongside private players to accelerate and expand deployments. In this context, Mr. Zogheib studies how the coexistence of private and public players affects competition and investment strategies. Mr. Zogheib shows that the competition from private operators weakens the position of public players, making it difficult for them to break even. A public player must then react either by increasing the price of its services or by reducing its investments, for example, by giving up covering the most remote and costly areas for network deployment. Competition between public and private players seems therefore counterproductive to achieve large coverage. Mr. Zogheib shows that, for example, the deployment of the infrastructure by a public monopoly would be a preferable solution, leading to wider network coverage. For fibre access networks, this is the choice made by some industrialised countries, such as Australia and New Zealand.

The third and final chapter of the thesis focuses on the role of privacy in the competition between digital platforms, when consumers can use a single service or several. In this context, Mr. Zogheib examines the competition between platforms, both on the prices they charge to consumers and on the level of privacy protection they offer. The level of privacy protection dictates to which extent a firm monetises the data it collects from its customers to improve the quality of service. Mr. Zogheib shows that firms adopt either a business model with high privacy protection and high prices, or a business model with low prices and the monetisation of consumer data. Mr. Zogheib then shows that a merger between platforms steers players towards the second business model, the one that is less protective of consumer privacy. The merger can therefore lead to significant harm for consumers in terms of privacy. Mr. Zogheib's research shows the importance of considering the role of consumer data in the competitive analysis of mergers in the digital sector.

The three topics addressed in the thesis are novel and important for the academic research in economics. However, they also provide valuable insights for competition policy and the regulation of network and digital industries.

The thesis has been awarded the Concurrences Prize by leading competition law and economics scholars. The first chapter has also been published independently in a peer-reviewed scientific journal, and the other two chapters have been presented at prestigious conferences.

It remains for me to wish Mr. Jean-Marc Zogheib the best of success in his future professional career.

Marc BOURREAU
Professor, Télécom Paris, Institut Polytechnique de Paris
Academic Co-Director of the CERRE

ACKNOWLEDGMENTS

I am particularly grateful to Marc Bourreau for having supervised my thesis. I learned a lot with him. Marc has a strong sense of pedagogy and is understanding. Moreover, he has been present at crucial moments. I really recommend him as a PhD supervisor!

I would also like to thank François Jeanjean, who was my supervisor at Orange during three years. François gave me the opportunity to pursue my research in the most efficient conditions and I am very grateful to him.

I would like to thank Maya Bacache, Axel Gautier, Edmond Baranès, Wilfried Sand-Zantman, François Jeanjean, and Marc Bourreau, who did me the honor of being part of the Jury of this thesis.

I would also like to thank Marc Lebourges who was the Director of the Europe- Economy division at the Regulatory Department of Orange before he retired for having been such an outstanding manager for the team. His advice and commitment were quite helpful.

I acknowledge my colleagues from Orange for being such a nice and pleasant team, with whom I regularly had the opportunity to discuss my research questions. I would like to particularly thank Julienne Liang, Laure Jaunaux, Karine Fourneron, Lionel De Rivières and Stéphane Ciriani.

During the last year of my thesis at Telecom Paris (but also before!), I spent a great time with Adrien Raizonville, Enrick Arnaud-Jouffray, Arrah-Marie Jo, Ambre Nicolle, Ángela Muñoz, Jordana Viotto, Ulrich Laitenberger, Vicente Lagos, Antoine Dubus, Martin Quinn, Yann Balgobin, Alexis Larousse, Morgane Cure, and numerous other colleages. I also benefited from the support of outstanding friends during this thesis: Xavier Pellet, Lucas Mahieux, Mélanie Magnier, and Christos Revelas.

Finally, I thank my parents, brother and sisters, for their formidable encouragement during this thesis. I am indebted to my wife Olga, for her forceful mental support. I am also indebted to my daughter Jeanne, who has been an outstanding motivation at the end of the thesis.

INTRODUCTION

1. A long tradition in the theory of industrial organisation has shown that firms'strategies (such as pricing, investment, innovation, mergers and acquisitions) can affect efficiency, either directly or indirectly, through changes of market structure. For this reason, public intervention may in some cases be called for, either ex ante (regulation) or ex post (via competition policy). In this respect, competition in network industries, such as telecommunications, energy, and digital services, is an essential topic of industrial organisation. Indeed, along with digital transformation, network industries are in continuous evolution and are a critical driver of economic growth.

2. Network industries are concentrated markets. They are characterised by the presence of network externalities, sunk costs and economies of scale and scope. Increasing returns to scale favor concentration and the emergence of large firms, which is why network industries are subject to strong scrutiny by competition authorities (CAs) and regulators.

3. In this book, I study firms' strategies in network industries. I first discuss firms' incentives to merge and merger policy. Second, I examine firms' investment strategies in new network infrastructures. Third, I consider the competitive framework of digital markets and the role of privacy in the competition between digital players.

1. Firms' incentives to merge and merger policy

4. Firms deploy strategies to reinforce their market power and their ability to invest and innovate. Among them, firms may decide to merge. Because mergers impact social welfare, most countries have laws requiring CAs to examine mergers. The role of CAs is to identify the main circumstances under which a merger should or should not be authorised. For instance, US and European CAs adopt a consumer-surplus standard, that is, a merger is considered anti-competitive if it reduces consumer surplus.

1.1. Welfare impact of mergers

5. Mergers can impact market competition in two ways. First, a merger may allow the merged firm to *unilaterally* exert market power and raise prices. Second,

a merger may favour *collusive* behaviours, and thereby increase prices.[1] In what follows, I focus on the unilateral effects of mergers.

6. **Unilateral effects.** The unilateral effects of mergers are linked to the increase in market power of the merged firms; absent efficiency gains, a merger harms consumers and society at large. Let us briefly review the main determinants of unilateral market power.

7. *Market concentration.* The lower the number of independent firms operating after a merger, the more likely it is to be detrimental to consumers. For instance, in the case of a merger to monopoly, the merged firm will not face competitive pressure in its pricing decision. In contrast, if the market is fragmented (i.e. each firm has a very low market share), the impact of a merger on the market will not be significant.[2]

8. *Market share.* Farrell and Shapiro (1990) determine that the lower the market share of the merging firms the less negative is the effect on prices. McAfee and Williams (1992) show that mergers resulting in a new largest firm and mergers that increase the size of the larger firm always reduce total welfare. Therefore, a merger that involves firms with low market shares is unlikely to have major adverse effects.

9. *Ease of entry.* The ease of entry can limit firms' ability to raise prices post merger. For instance, firms that may find it unprofitable to enter the industry at pre-merger prices could decide to enter if the merger is price-increasing. To avoid further entry, post-merger prices might then not rise (or if not, an increase would be only transitory). However, the effect of the ease of entry on restraining market power depends on sunk costs; the higher the sunk costs that an entrant has to incur, the greater the scope for a price increase.[3]

10. Other important indicators of market power are the characteristics of demand (e.g. presence of high switching costs, and in general, a low demand elasticity) and buyer power (e.g. a high degree of concentration of the buyers so that upstream market power is constrained through the threat of withdrawing orders from one seller and giving them to another).

---

[1] In US merger policy, collusive effects are also called *coordinated* effects; a merger is evaluated according to the "substantial lessening of competition" test, i.e. the risk that the merger can reduce competition and raise prices. The EU merger policy employs a dominance test, where *joint dominance* is associated with pro-collusive effects.

[2] A measure of market concentration can be obtained with the Herfindhal-Hirschman Index (HHI). It is one screening device for unilateral effects of mergers: all things being equal, one should worry more about a merger in an industry that is highly concentrated than about one that happens in a fragmented industry.

[3] Merger policy (EU Merger Regulation, 2004; US Merger Guidelines, 2010) clearly takes into account the impact of entry when evaluating the impact of a merger. For instance, in the US Merger Guidelines (p. 28, Sec. 9), it is stated that:

> A merger is not likely to enhance market power if entry into the market is so easy that the merged firm and its remaining rivals in the market, either unilaterally or collectively, could not profitably raise price or otherwise reduce competition compared to the level that would prevail in the absence of the merger.

11. **Efficiency gains**. Efficiency gains may offset the enhanced market power of the merging firms, in which case the merger increases welfare (Williamson, 1968). Efficiency gains can be of different nature. They can be due to the existence of economies of scope (i.e. lower costs due to joint production) and economies of scale (i.e. a proportionate saving in costs gained by an increased level of production). Efficiencies may also arise from synergies in R&D, marketing activities, cost savings in administration, and rationalisation of distribution.

12. CAs require efficiency gains to be merger-specific. The European Commission (EC) requires efficiencies to be verifiable, merger-specific, and beneficial to consumers, the three being cumulative conditions.[4]

13. **Merger remedies**. In order to accept a merger, CAs may require remedies by the merging parties. Merger remedies are of two types: (i) structural remedies modify the allocation of property rights, while (ii) behavioural remedies constrain the merging firms property rights.

14. *Structural remedies*. CAs might require merger remedies in the form of a divestment of assets in order to avoid (post-merger) potential anti-competitive effects. The divested assets can be acquired by an entrant or an existing competitor. One issue is to ensure that the divested asset acquirer will be an active competitor in the market.

15. *Behavioural remedies*. They mainly consist of commitments that aim at guaranteeing a level playing field for non-merging firms (for instance, by ensuring the purchase or use of some key assets or technologies owned by the merged firm).[5]

16. Ensuring the effectiveness of merger remedies is an issue for CAs. In a report on the anti-competitiveness of mergers (EC, 2017b), the EC questioned the effectiveness of its remedy policy and expressed its clear preference for structural remedies. In light of the merger wave in the telecommunications industry, it is argued that, in absence of structural remedies, many mergers could not have been approved, given the high level of concentration in this network industry.

17. Notably, the telecommunications industry is subject to competition policy but also to strong sector-specific regulation. In what follows, I focus on competition policy aspects.

1.2. Competition policy and mergers in network industries: the case of telecommunications.

18. Since the liberalisation of telecommunications in the 1990s, in order to encourage entry and innovation, CAs have primarily cared about limiting the market power exerted by the former monopolists. CAs have paid special attention to the issue of unilateral effects after a merger between mobile network operators (MNOs). The telecommunications market is very concentrated due to high entry barriers

---

4 In other words, efficiency gains need to be fully documented, that is, (i) synergies that could be achieved through less anticompetitive means (e.g. via internal growth) would not be recognised, and (ii) savings on fixed costs would not be accepted as they would not lead to lower prices.

5 Behavioral remedies can also be in a contractual form. For example, the merging parties can be obliged to license a given technology to a rival (i.e. a "quasi-structural" remedy).

for new players that would like to roll-out network infrastructures (mobile or fixed). In particular, a significant entry barrier exists for mobile, because spectrum, which is an essential input for mobile operators, is a scarce resource, auctioned periodically and at a high price. This is why in the EU, the EC has encouraged the entry of mobile virtual network operators (MVNOs).

19. To guarantee a competitive environment, a challenge for CAs is to enforce an effective merger policy. In relation to this, let us discuss some important four-to-three mergers between mobile operators investigated by the EC.

20. In 2014, the H3G/O2 merger[6] in Ireland was conditionally approved by the EC. To mitigate potential loss of competitive pressure due to this four-to-three merger, H3G negotiated a set of remedies: ensuring the entry of new MVNOs, the continuation of the network sharing agreement with Eircom,[7] the provision of wholesale network access to at least two MVNOs with an option for one of them to become an MNO by acquiring some of the company's spectrum capacity.

21. More recently, EC merger policy has become stricter, especially in terms of remedies. In 2016, the EC refused the (four-to-three) merger between Telefonica and H3G in the UK[8]. On top of competitive concerns over this merger (e.g. the risk of lower investment in infrastructures, the potential elimination of MNVOs), the EC found that the remedies proposed by H3G were not sufficient to offset these serious concerns. In 2015, TeliaSonera and Telenor aborted their merger project[9] because of the extent of merger remedies required by the EC, in particular, the entry of a new competitor.[10]

22. Telenor and TeliaSonera's main argument in favour of their merger was that it would increase their ability and capacity to invest in new network infrastructures. However, the EC challenged the view that mergers, or a lower number of competitors, impact positively investment. Using a theoretical framework, Motta and Tarantino (2021) show that a merger might increase total investments and consumer surplus only if it entails sufficient (merger-specific) efficiency gains. Bourreau and Jullien (2018) show that a merger may lead to more investment in coverage, absent any synergies. Using an empirical framework, Houngbonon and Jeanjean (2017) determine that in the long run, investment eventually falls with the number of operators. Genakos, Valletti, and Verboven (2018) find that more concentrated markets lead to higher end user prices and increase investment per mobile operator.

23. Firms may choose to expand not only to their respective domestic markets, but also to foreign markets by acquiring foreign companies, that is, through cross-border mergers.

---

6 *Hutchison 3G UK/Telefonica Ireland* (Case M.6992, C 264, 13.08.2014, OJ L 24).

7 Eircom was the third and smallest network operator. It had a network sharing agreement with 02.

8 *Hutchison 3G UK/Telefonica UK*(Case M.7612, C 357, 29.09.2016, OJ L 24).

9 *TeliaSonera Denmark/Telenor Denmark* (Case M.7419, C316, 24.09.2015, OJ L 24).

10 For more details on the impact of mergers in telecommunications, see Ian Streule and Alessia Marrazzo, "Claims for damages due to abuse of dominance rely heavily on identifying the correct counter factual case" (Analysys Mason and Lear, 2017) <http://ec.europa.eu/competition/publications/reports/kd0417233enn.pdf>.

1.3. Cross-border mergers

24. Cross-border mergers (CBMs) are deals between foreign companies and domestic firms. In a changing environment impacted by globalisation, there has been an increasing trend of CBM activity. Between 2008 and 2012, the number of mergers in Europe decreased while the number of CBMs increased (Figure 1a).[11]

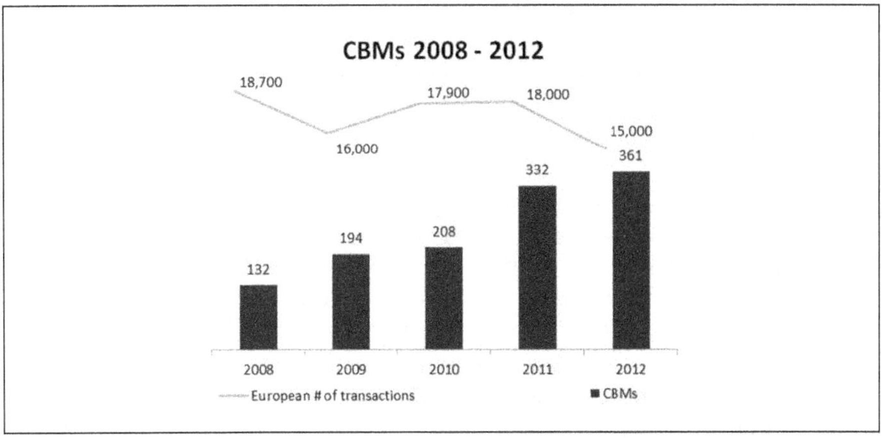

(a)

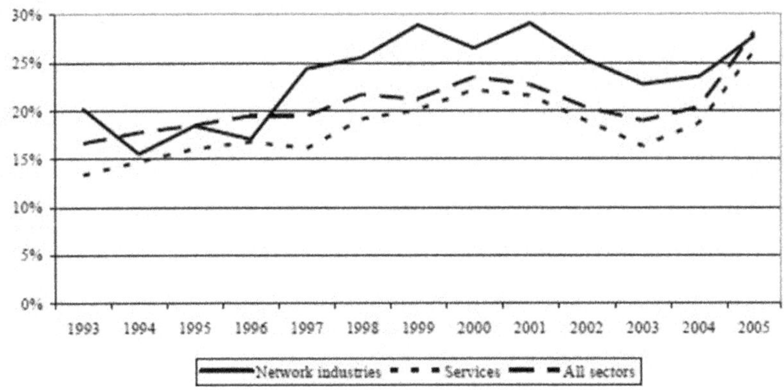

(b)

Figure 1 – (a) Mergers and CBMs in EU and EEA from 2008 to 2012; (b) Share of CBMs in network industries (as % of total number of mergers).

25. In the literature, it is considered that CBMs are primarily undertaken to gain access to complementary firm-specific assets (Nocke and Yeaple, 2008), capabilities that are non-mobile across countries (Nocke and Yeaple, 2007), or country-specific assets (Norback and Persson, 2007).

---

11 Source: Bech-Bruun, European Commission, and Lexidale (2016).

26. CBMs can serve as a tool to achieve policy objectives such as the market integration of a regional market. This is in this context that in the EU, the Cross-Border Mergers directive (CBMD, 2005/56/EC) was implemented. The CBMD created a framework for CBMs and aimed to facilitating them. More recently, there has been a proposal for further simplification of CBM procedures.[12]

27. *Cross-border merger and network industries in the EU.* With the liberalisation phase of network industries in the 1990s and the EC's will to build a single market across the EU, CBMs in network industries have become a high-order issue. In Figure (1b), it can be observed that between 1993 and 2005, CBMs in network industries experienced a positive trend.[13]

28. In a study of the performance of network industries providing services of general economic interest (EC, 2006), it has been considered that in the context of market integration, CBMs are "likely to lead to spillovers and to the dissemination of technological know-how" (p. 51). In other words, CBMs are viewed as a mean to enhance market integration of network industries and to generate potentially high market-level synergies in the EU internal market.

29. The internal market is often invoked in support of calls for more consolidation in network industries, leading to the emergence of stronger European-level players. However, it does not imply that all consolidation plans are cross-border. In addition, network industries are quite concentrated, meaning that efforts towards market consolidation could often raise competitive concerns.

30. To conquer markets, firms may decide to merge not only in their respective domestic markets (i.e. in-market merger) but also across borders. However, a firm's decision to merge can have anti-competitive effects. In response, merger policy needs to set adapted rules that ensure a fair competition environment. The first chapter examines the extent to which merger policy impacts a firm's decision to merge in-market vs cross-border.

2. Investments in new network infrastructures

31. To expand, firms may need to invest in new network infrastructures. Firms' investment strategies have to be considered with regard to the liberalisation of network industries during the 1990s and early 2000s. A key question is how the regulatory framework has adapted to this changing environment.

32. This question is studied in what follows in the context of the telecommunications sector.

---

12 See the amendment of Directive (EU) 2017/1132 (22 March 2019). https://data.consilium.europa.eu/doc/document/ST-7426-2019-INIT/en/pdf

13 Source: EC (2006).

2.1. Regulatory framework in network industries

33. Since the 1990s, the telecommunications sector has profoundly evolved from regulated monopolies to oligopolistic competition. The services offered have diversified (e.g. with the introduction of fixed and mobile broadband access services) and are continuously changing. As a result, the regulatory framework has also to evolve. For instance, the presence of scale and scope economies and of network effects has led to calls for the introduction of asymmetric regulations to control the market power of incumbents (e.g. the unbundling of the local loop through which each incumbent telecommunications operator makes its local network available to other telecommunications operators).

34. *Evolution of the regulatory framework.* The regulatory framework has evolved through three major phases.[14]

35. The first phase was the liberalisation phase, going from regulated monopolies to service-based competition (i.e. when entrants use the incumbent's infrastructure to provide their services); it took place in the 1990's in Europe. A crucial issue during this phase was that entrant operators faced significant entry barriers. Indeed, due to consumer switching costs, the incumbent operator controlling essential facilities (the local loop), and the potential for entry deterrence (through aggressive competition), the challenge of regulation was to promote entry and competition. To reduce entry barriers, several regulatory measures were taken – among them, the privatisation of the incumbent operator and the rebalancing of tariffs with cost-oriented retail charges. By regulating access charges, a move towards service-based competition followed.

36. The second phase was a transition phase from service-based to infrastructure-based competition (i.e. when entrants use their own network infrastructure). The concept of the *ladder of investment* (Cave, 2006) describes this transition phrase well. The basic principle of this approach is gradually offering potential entrants different levels of access to the incumbent's network. Entrants begin with acquiring access at a level that requires little investment to provide their services. Then, as the entrants' consumer bases grow, they are incentivised to invest in the network elements necessary to bypass this first level of access. The entrants then "climb" the investment ladder, and acquire access at the next level, and so on. The ladder of investment approach has been widely adopted by CAs in Europe. Bacache, Bourreau and Gaudin (2014) provide an empirical analysis of the ladder of investment.[15]

37. The third phase is characterised by infrastructure-based competition (i.e. at the top of the ladder of investment). In this phase, regulation is first concerned with the transition from old technology networks (copper local loop) to new technology networks (fibre). In this context, there have been intense debates in the EU on the impact of the regulation of the unbundling of the local loop on the incentives to invest in fibre.[16] Moreover, regulation is concerned with infrastructure-sharing and its impact on investment and competition, because infrastructure-sharing can

---

[14] For a more comprehensive treatment of the regulatory framework in the telecommunications, see Bourreau (2016).

[15] According to ARCEP, "the development of competition in France since 1998 is a good illustration of the theory of the ladder of investment". See ARCEP (p. 36, 2007).

[16] For a formal treatment of this question, see Bourreau, Cambini and Dogan (2012, 2014).

be a way to lower investment costs (thereby avoiding inefficient duplication of networks) and foster infrastructure-based competition. In the EU, the EC has supported co-investment agreements insofar as they are believed to allow better fibre coverage of a territory.[17] The new regulatory code explicitly considers co-investment as a form of access.

38. Regulation faces a trade-off between an access-based model and an infrastructure-sharing model (Bourreau, Cambini and Hoernig, 2018). These two modes of regulatory intervention raise the question of how to promote competition in geographic areas where rolling out a network is very costly.[18]

2.2. Universal Service

39. Universal service is the general principle that all users should have access to a range of basic but good-quality services at affordable prices. The concept of universal service is central in network industries (e.g. telecommunications, electricity, water), where the costs of serving certain categories of users may exceed the associated revenues. Governments and regulators pursue the goal of universal service for several reasons, among them, equity and economic development.

40. Before the liberalisation of telecommunications, restrictions were imposed on regulated monopolies in the form of universal service obligations (USOs), such as restrictions on prices or the obligation to offer certain services in outlying geographic areas (Gautier and Wauthy, 2010). The losses caused by these restrictions were usually financed through large cross-subsidies, in particular from long-distance and business services. The opening of competition and changes in technology led to the questioning of the sustainability of these USOs.

41. In the EU, the Universal Service Directive (2002) is the legislation that defines universal service for telecommunications.[19] To take into account the evolution of technology, the Universal Service Directive was revised in 2009. In particular, this revision specifies that access to the public communications network should support "functional access to the internet, taking into account prevailing technologies, used by the majority of subscribers, and technological feasibility".[20] As a result, it gives EU Member States a wider scope to define the exact terms of USOs.[21]

42. *Broadband and USOs.* A key issue is the inclusion of broadband under USOs. The main arguments in favour of USOs for broadband are (i) the importance of overcoming the digital divide, and (ii) the positive role that broadband can play in encouraging social and economic development. However, including broadband in USOs may have negative effects. Indeed, it could distort markets, harm

---

17 See EC (2010).

18 The issue of cooperation between firms to deploy a very high capacity network is all the more relevant following the COVID-19 crisis. For more details, see CERRE (2020b).

19 Council Directive 2002/22/EC of the European Parliament on universal service and users' rights relating to electronic communications networks and services (Universal Service Directive), 7 March 2009, OJ L 108.

20 Council Directive 2009/136/EC of the European Parliament, 25 April 2009, OJ L 108.

21 Various mechanisms exist to ensure the affordability of universal services for citizens. For instance, EU Members States use mechanisms such as uniform pricing or price caps. See CERRE (2015).

competition and reduce private investment in network infrastructures, particularly in outlying areas. In addition, other means are available to foster investment: for instance, State aid from Member States or EU funding (e.g. the European Fund for Strategic Investments (EFSI)).[22] Gautier and Wauthy (2010) investigate how USOs, by way of pricing restrictions, alter competition between firms in prices and coverage.

43. The discussion on the extent of USOs leads to the more general question of the role of public intervention in network industries.

2.3. Role of public intervention in network industries

44. Opening the telecommunications sector to competition has been accompanied by measures to provide a universal service. However, beyond the USO framework, public intervention may take other forms. For example, public authorities may intervene if they consider that mechanisms in place are not sufficient to ensure the desired coverage of the territory.

45. To foster investment in network infrastructures, public intervention can occur via two channels: (i) a regulatory channel (i.e. to incentivise private operators to invest more), and (ii) a financial channel (i.e. public investment in network infrastructures). The objective of public intervention is to fix possible market failures. However, there is the issue is of avoid the distortion of competition.

46. The impact of public intervention has to be considered with respect to the geographical market conditions of a territory, that is, the area type. Three types of areas are commonly identified. First, *white areas* are regions where it is not profitable to invest in a network infrastructure. Following public policy objectives, public authorities may then legitimately intervene. Second, *black areas* are regions where infrastructure competition (between two or more private operators) is viable. In this case, public intervention is not justifiable and may be harmful. Third, *grey areas* are regions where there is only one network operator and where the probability that a competing network will be deployed is small. In these areas, it can, for instance, happen that the network operator has significant market power and provides a low-quality service with high prices, or that some portions of the territory are not adequately covered. Depending on market conditions, public intervention may then be necessary.

47. *Framework of public intervention in the EU.* Public funds, or State aid, have supported the deployment of broadband infrastructure in Europe since the early 2000s. Particularly since 2010, a growing trend towards the use of public funds by the EC and Member States to foster broadband deployment has been observed.[23] This trend is all the more important as the EC and Member States adopted ambitious targets for a Gigabit Society.

48. Because State aid may distort competition (as a particular company receives the benefit of State aid and others do not), it requires the application of a "balancing

---

22 See European Parliament (2016).

23 For a theoretical contribution, see Jullien, Pouyet and Sand-Zantman (2010).

test" to keep any harmful effects to an absolute minimum in order to achieve the intended outcomes. If the conditions of the balancing test are not met, the proposed State aid will be unlawful.[24] Importantly, Article 108 of the Treaty of Lisbon requires Member States to notify proposed State aid measures to the EC for review. However, the 2014 General Block Exemption Regulation (GBER) contains provisions to exempt broadband State aid projects from notification requirements.[25]

49. Other forms of public funding fall outside the State aid regime: for example, if public funds relate to *services of general economic interest* (SGEI), within the meaning of Article 117(2) of the Treaty of Lisbon. Following the Altmark judgment of the European Court of Justice (ECJ),[26] these services can be compensated with public funding, which does not constitute State aid when some cumulative conditions are met.[27] The framework of SGEI in the EU is further tackled in the EU guidelines for the application of State aid rules concerning the rapid deployment of broadband networks (EC, 2013). The EC considers that in areas where private investors have already invested in a broadband network infrastructure and are providing competitive broadband services, setting up a parallel competitive and public broadband infrastructure would not be considered as an SGEI, thanks to Article 106(2) TFEU (31). However, the EU guidelines state that

> Where it can be demonstrated that private investors are not in a position to provide in the near future adequate broadband coverage to all citizens, a public service compensation may be granted to an undertaking entrusted with the operation of an SGEI. (par. 20)

50. Thus, the EC's objective is to set up effective rules allowing public intervention to foster investment in poorly served areas while trying to maintain a fair competition environment.[28]

51. Public intervention in network industries is hotly debated, particularly in the aftermath of the COVID-19 crisis. Legitimate considerations relative to the extent of universal service have to be balanced with rules that ensure an efficient market economy. On the one hand, public investments can compensate for market failures in remote areas where private investment would not occur or would take

---

24 See Article 107(1) of the Treaty of Lisbon for the criteria that determine whether a measure represents State aid.

25 Four conditions have to be met: (i) the total funds do not exceed 70 million, (ii) the area defined is a white area, (iii) the recipient is subject to "the widest possible passive and active wholesale access", including physical unbundling of next-generation access (NGA) services and access to duct, and (iv) the funds are allocated by means of competitive tender and subject to clawback provisions.

26 This judgment was precised by the EC and is relative to the application of EU State aid rules for compensating SGEI delivery. See See *Altmark judgment* (Case C280/00, 24.07.2003, OJ L 169).

27 The conditions are (p. 15-16): "(i) the recipient undertaking must have public service obligations and the obligations must be clearly defined; (ii) the parameters for calculating the compensation must be objective, transparent and established in advance; (iii) the compensation cannot exceed what is necessary to cover all or part of the costs incurred in the discharge of the public service obligations, taking into account the relevant receipts and a reasonable profit; (iv) where the undertaking which is to discharge public service obligations is not chosen pursuant to a public procurement procedure which would allow for the selection of the tenderer capable of providing those services at the least cost to the community, the level of compensation needed must be determined on the basis of an analysis of the costs of a typical well-run company." See EC (2011).

28 For a more comprehensive treatment of the framework of State aid for broadband in Europe (and more broadly the framework of public intervention), see Bourreau, Feasey and Nicolle (2020).

too long to materialise. On the other hand, public investments may distort market competition and affect negatively private investment.

52. The extent to which public investment may crowd out private investment in network industries is addressed in Chapter 2.

3. Competition in digital markets

53. The digital economy covers all business, economic, social and cultural activities that are supported by the web and other digital communication and information technologies. Digital technologies have lowered the cost of collecting, distributing and using data, thus reducing search costs. This evolution has led to the emergence of new business models that involve the exploitation of user data. New concerns in terms of privacy and competition have arisen (e.g. markets dominated by a few ecosystems and platforms).[29] The emergence of the digital economy therefore raises new challenges for competition policy. As stated in a recent report commissioned by the EC (Cremer, Montjoye and Schweitzer, 2019):

> The fundamental changes that the data and platform economy are bringing about challenge many of the other types of rules and regulations which have been tailored to deal with "old world" problems. (p. 14)

3.1. Data: a new type of economic asset

54. Big data, which refers to a process that is used when traditional data mining techniques cannot uncover the insights and meaning of the underlying data, appears to be an essential element of the digital economy. The amount of information generated on a daily basis is increasing exponentially (Figure 2).[30]

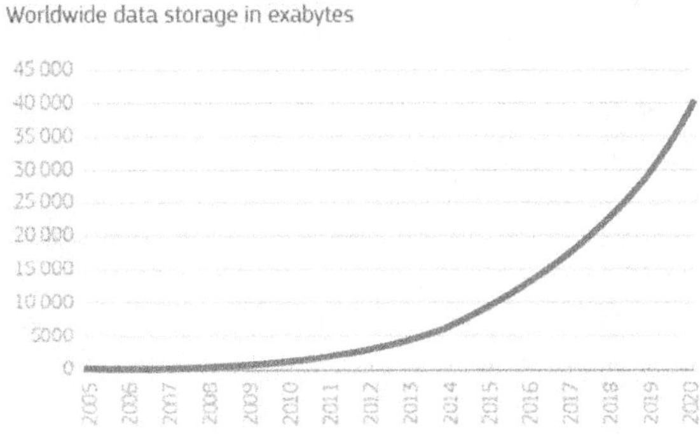

Figure 2 – Global expansion of data

29 By the end of September 2018, the largest firms in the world by market capitalisation (Apple, Amazon, Microsoft and Alphabet) were in the digital industry.

30 Source: International Data Corporation Digital University Study (https://blogs.idc.com/).

55. As a result, data is becoming a new driver of productivity and innovation. Firms that adopt data-driven decision-making have been found to have a 5-6% higher output and productivity (Brynjolfsson, Hitt and Kim, 2011). Firms can use big data analytics to help them develop new products and services, re-engineer their business processes, and gain clearer insights into customer needs.

56. **Mechanisms of value creation in the data eco-system.** Let us decompose the data value chain into four categories.[31]

57. *Data generators.* They are the primary source of data (e.g. users browsing the internet). Data can be generated *passively*, that is, when users generating data are not necessarily aware that their action is providing information that is collected by another entity; for instance, when a driver uses a mapping application. It can also be generated *actively*, that is, when users sign up to a social network and provide some of their information. Because the information created is valuable to data services, data generators may be able to benefit by "monetising" this information. A common example is the business model of advertiser-supported websites that allow consumers to use services for free while the business then use the information provided for targeted advertising purposes.

58. *Data services.* Data becomes an output when it is processed and analysed (i.e. structuring, storage, adaptation). This is at the step of the value chain where "bottlenecks" can arise. In digital markets that are characterised by a trend towards concentration, strong network effects, and economies of scale, competitive concerns may arise. For instance, the more data an incumbent firm collects, the better and more efficient its services may become, thereby reinforcing market dominance. For instance, as more users use a search engine, more feedback is received, which makes the search engine more efficient in providing customised results for users, thereby strengthening the search engine market position.

59. *Data business users.* Firms and public entities can use the collected and processed data to improve performance and market strategies (for marketing, launching a new product). The ability to use efficiently big data analytics rests in particular on the regulatory framework regarding privacy, data protection and security. In this context, the EU implemented the General Data Protection Regulation (GDPR) in 2018. The GDPR is a European regulation on data protection and privacy for all individuals and citizens of the EU and the EEA.[32]

60. *End users.* The last group of the value chain are the downstream buyers such as consumers and business customers related to firms that have used the processed data. End users can benefit from tailored offers, price reductions, or better quality

---

31 To do so, I build on an EC report on the data economy (EC, 2017a). This categorisation is done for the ease of exposition. In reality, categories may overlap.

32 Council Regulation (EU) 2016/679 of 27 April 2016 on the protection of natural persons with regard to the processing of personal data and on the free movement of such data, and repealing Directive 95/46/EC (General Data Protection Regulation), OJ L 119. The objective of the GDPR is essentially to give individuals control over their personal information, thereby simplifying the regulatory environment for business by harmonising the regulation within the EU. It contains provisions and requirements on the processing of personal information of "data subjects".

service (e.g. the users of Waze sharing information about traffic while driving). However, these benefits may come with some costs: on top of security and privacy risks, end users can be more vulnerable to exploitative pricing practices (i.e. price discrimination). Indeed, sellers can exploit user data to get a more precise profile and charge a price that is closer to the user's willingness to pay. For example, Montes, Sand-Zantman, and Valletti (2018) provide an analysis of the impact of personalised pricing, using consumer data, and show that a move from uniform to personalised prices may decreases total welfare, but that consumers benefit from this move.

61. **Necessity of a regulatory framework on data**. In digital markets where the exploitation of user information is key, the regulatory framework has to address two main potential market failures.

62. First, there are privacy and security issues: this stems from the potential inability of consumers to assess the extent to which they are exposed to a risk because of the information they provide. Second, it may be difficult for market forces to make socially optimal use of data as it is not possible to fully internalise data spill-over effects. This comes from the non-rivalry nature of data which means that it can be used multiple times by multiple users without decreasing its value. For example, data that has been collected for marketing purposes may be reused to improve healthcare research at a minimal cost. If these potential spill-over effects are not considered, there is a risk of undersupply of data analysis compared to what would be socially optimal.

63. The role of public authorities is to address these market failures. In this respect, regulators face a trade-off between fostering the digital economy and guaranteeing an efficient data protection policy.

64. The rise of big data has made data a new type of economic asset. This new asset is essential when considering competition in digital markets.

3.2. Key features of digital markets

65. Let us elaborate on some key characteristics of digital markets.

66. *Large returns to scale*. The cost of production of a digital service is mainly fixed and therefore involves economies of scale (Shapiro and Varian, 1998). For instance, once a search engine has been developed, it can serve a huge number of users at a low cost. In addition, with increasing returns to scale, two competing firms supplying a homogenous product cannot cover their costs. Indeed, to cover their total costs, firms would have to price above marginal costs but they would find it profitable to lower prices to steal the rival's consumers; entry in a market dominated by an incumbent would then be difficult. As analysed by Shapiro and Varian (1998), there are only two sustainable market structures for digital goods: the dominant firm model (monopoly) or the differentiated product market.

67. *Network effects*. Network effects arise when the utility of a consumer using a service increases as the number of users increases. Network effects are of particular importance as digital markets are often multi-sided, that is, when a *platform* acts as an intermediary between two or more distinct user groups. Network effects can be same-sided (e.g. new users joining a platform as the number of users

increases) or cross-sided (e.g. more advertisers signing up to a platform on one side as the user base grows on the other side). Network effects are another source of increasing returns to scale: network effects profit large incumbents and favour market concentration. They raise entry barriers as, on top of supplying better service quality (or lower price) than the incumbent, the entrant has to incentivise the incumbent's users to migrate to its own services. Network effects may therefore give rise to an incumbency advantage. The size of this advantage depends on the possibility of multi-homing, data portability, and data interoperability.[33]

68. *Impact of data.* As discussed above, data has become an essential input of many online services and production processes. The ability to exploit data to provide innovative services is thus a critical competitive parameter. Dominant firms, which are bottlenecks on user data enjoy a competitive advantage. Along with the presence of large economies of scale and the prevalence of network effects, the development of data collection and usage may strengthen the market power of leading companies in digital markets.[34]

69. Digital markets are also characterised by the presence of strong economies of scope arising from the possession of data, the idea being that once a firm offer a service, it becomes more efficient at offering others (e.g. a multi-service firm designing a new service using an individual's data), thereby favouring the dominance of incumbent firms.

70. When data brings a significant competitive advantage to their owners, firms will need to collect and exploit more data in order to remain competitive. To keep their competitive advantage, firms may have incentives to engage in anti-competitive conducts. This is why in the digital economy, the enforcement of an effective competition policy is a challenge for CAs.

3.3. Enforcement of competition policy in digital markets

71. Digital markets raise new challenges for competition policy. An issue is to adapt classical concepts of competition policy to the digital economy. Let us discuss some of these concepts.[35]

72. *Consumer welfare standard.* The application of the consumer welfare criterion may be adapted in digital markets where prices often play a different role compared to more traditional industries. The analysis of consumer harm has focused on potential short-run and price-based effects. In the digital economy, it may be more accurate to evaluate the effects on quality and innovation. This is, for instance, relevant in

---

33 Multi-Homing is when a user signs up to not only one service but to several services (e.g. Netflix and HBO). Data portability refers to the ability of users to transfer the data that a platform has collected about them. The EU (GDPR) has introduced a limited right to data portability (Article 20) as a means to avoid data-driven lock-ins. Data (or protocol) interoperability ensures that two systems can fully work together and that complementary services can be provided. For a more comprehensive treatment of data with respect to competition law, see Duch-Brown, Marten and Mueller-Langer (2017).

34 For a detailed analysis of the prevalence of market power in digital markets, and more generally, on data and competition policy, see the joint report Autorité de la Concurrence and Bundeskartellamt (2016).

35 I build on Cremer, Montjoye and Schweitzer (2019).

platform-to-consumers (P2C) markets where services are offered at a free price and where no price effects exist.[36] Moreover, there may be a risk of under-enforcement of competition policy caused by the persistence of market power in digital markets. This is why dominant firms' market strategies that reduce competitive pressure should receive attention, even in absence of clearly identified consumer harm.

73. *Market definition.* Due to the prevalence of network effects, it can be complicated to give a clear market definition, especially in multi-sided markets. For instance, the classic small but significant and non-transitory increase in price (SSNIP) test[37] is hardly applicable; on top of the issue of free pricing, increasing one price without modifying the price on the other side does not really make sense. The interdependence of the sides is then crucial. Moreover, digital markets are driven by innovation and are continuously changing, as are market boundaries. This suggests that less emphasis should be put on the analysis of market definition (Baranes and Cosnita-Langlais, 2016).

74. *Measuring market power.* The concept of market power is used to identify cases of market dominance. CAs usually measure market power by using market shares. However, due to network effects, prices do not necessarily represent the value of the service to the consumers or to the firms that are selling them; as a result, the market shares may not be a good indicator to evaluate market power in digital markets.[38] In fact, market power can exist even in an apparently fragmented market. This kind of market power is linked to the concept of "intermediation power" in the multi-sided platform framework.[39] Moreover, if some data that provides a strong competitive advantage is not available to entrants, it can lead to market dominance. Along with intermediation power, an evaluation of market power should consider the issue of the replicability of data.

75. The enforcement of competition policy in digital markets is therefore a hot topic to which CAs are seeking to respond.[40] In this respect, the *Digital Markets Act* (DMA) could be a stepping stone.[41] This regulation is intended to ensure a fair competition environment in presence of online platforms acting as "gatekeepers". A digital firm is designated as a gatekeeper if it has (i) a strong economic position in the EU internal market, (ii) a strong intermediation position, and (iii) a stable market position over time. The DMA is expected to benefit to all economic actors (businesses, consumers, platforms, start-ups) and to drive innovation.[42] For instance, it will forbid

---

36 Other relevant examples are platform-to-business (P2B) and business-to-business (B2B) platforms where the degree of innovation determines the level of productivity of the economy.

37 In competition law, the test of small but significant and non-transitory increase in price (SSNIP) is used to define the relevant market in a consistent way.

38 *ibid.* note 34.

39 For more details on the concept of intermediation power, see Schweitzer, Haucap, Kerber and Welker (2018).

40 Caffarra, Crawford, & Valletti (2020) highlighted the issue of "killer acquistions" in digital markets. The basic idea is that an established firm could acquire an innovative entrant firm without developing its innovation afterwards. For more details on the issue of mergers in digital markets, see CERRE (2020a).

41 See COM/2020/842 final, Digital Markets Act (15 December 2020). The Digital Markets Act, along with the Digital Services Act, are the backbones of the EU digital strategy.

42 Varian (2021) examines several competition policy issues related to bigtechs firms ("Seven deadly sins of tech?"). He argues that, overall, competition among digital firms is working well and is positive for consumer welfare and the whole economy.

the gatekeeper's platform from treating its own service more favourably in ranking than competing services offered by third parties on the gatekeeper's platform.[43]

76. The advent of digital markets is related to the rise of big data through which data has become a new economic asset. Digital markets have key characteristics that affects firms' market strategies as well as the framework of competition policy. Along with price competition, firms also compete in the collection and use of user data, that is, information disclosure. However, this could raise user privacy concerns.

77. In Chapter 3, I examine the impact of competition between firms in prices and information disclosure levels.

4. Summary of chapters

4.1. Merging In-Market vs Cross-Border: The Impact of Merger Policy

78. Chapter 1[44] studies how merger policy affects the choice between in-market and cross-border merging. I build a model where four firms compete in a regional market, which has two markets: a home market and a foreign market. The two markets are segmented and of same size, with two firms in each. The merger policy, set at the regional level, is defined by the probability that a merger is cleared. After observing the merger policy, a firm chooses between a CBM or an in-market merger (IMM). Thereafter, it may decide to separate from its merger partner, depending on the merger outcome. An IMM is always profitable and efficient (but still subject to competitive concerns) while a CBM has a certain probability of being profitable. In the case where the firm chooses to separate from its merger partner after a CBM, undoing the merger may involve an exit through an IMM, contingent on merger policy. In a benchmark case where an exit-by-merger is impossible, I find that a stricter (-more lenient) merger policy shifts firms' decisions towards CBMs (-IMMs). Conversely, if it is possible to exit by merger, I find that the merger policy also affects the incentives to merge cross-border by lowering (or increasing) exit barriers. This modifies the trade-off between both merger types insofar as the merger policy affects the incentives to merge in-market and cross-border differently. This analysis then implies that if the merger policy were very strict and market-level synergies were low (i.e. the payoff from merging would be low), firms would ultimately not merge at all. From a policy point of view, these results suggest that the merger policy should consider subsequent mergers triggered by an initial decision to merge, which here corresponds to the scenario of an exit-by-merger after a failed CBM.

---

43 In this context, Alphabet (Google), which has the profile of a gatekeeping platform, took over the consumer electronics and fitness company Fitbit. This acquisition has been cleared by the European Commission after an in-depth investigation and is "conditional on full compliance with a commitments package offered by Google". See Google/Fitbit (Case M.9660, C 194, 17.12.2020, OJ L 24).

44 This chapter was published in the *Revue d'Economie Industrielle, 2018, no 4, p. 107-129*

4.2. Public vs Private Investments in Network Industries

79. Chapter 2[45] examines the impact of competition between a private firm and public firms on prices and investment in new infrastructures. I build a model where firms decide simultaneously on prices for their product, and on coverage of a territory with a new network technology. The private firm maximises its profit, while public firms maximise the sum of their profits and consumer surplus, all subject to budget constraints. Two scenarios of public intervention are considered: a national public firm and local public firms. The national public firm charges a uniform price across the areas it has covered while the price charged by local public firms depends on their location, that is, whether they are in high-cost or low-cost areas.

80. In a monopoly benchmark, I find that the private firm charges the monopoly price and covers up to a – geographical – area where the monopoly profit is equal to the marginal cost of investment. The national public firm never charges more than the monopoly price; it sets a price such that it cross-subsidises between low-cost and high-cost areas, which allows it to cover a larger share of the country than the private firm. Local public firms, which charge prices contingent on the investment cost in their own area, charge no more than the monopoly price and cover the same areas as the private firm.

81. In a mixed duopoly where the national public firm has invested more than the private firm, I find that prices are strategic complements for the private firm and are strategic substitutes for the national public firm. A larger overlap between the private firm's and the public firm's networks drives firms' prices up. In the equilibrium of the coverage-price game, total coverage by the national public firm is lower than the benchmark. Competition leads the private firm to set lower prices than the benchmark, while the public firm may charge higher prices than the benchmark; this can be explained by the competition from the private firm, which makes it harder to sustain low prices.

82. In a mixed duopoly where the local public firms have invested more than the private firm, I find that a larger overlap between the private firm's network and the local public firms' networks leads to a higher price by the private firm and lower prices by the local public firms. In the equilibrium of the coverage-price game, total coverage is the same as the benchmark. The private firm sets a lower price than the benchmark, while the local public firms set higher prices.

4.3. Privacy, Competition and Multi-Homing

83. Chapter 3[46] examines the impact of competition between firms in prices and information disclosure levels. In a two-sided market model, two firms supply a horizontally differentiated service to consumers on one side, and sell consumer information to a monopoly data broker on the other side. Consumers observe the

[45] This chapter is a joint work with Marc Bourreau.

[46] This chapter is a joint work with Marc Bourreau.

level of disclosure in which firms engage and their prices before deciding which service to patronise and how much personal information to provide.

84. I find that firms adopt two types of business strategies due to a trade-off between the collection of consumer information, the level of information provision, and consumer valuations. If consumer valuations are sufficiently low, firms engage in the disclosure of consumer information (low-privacy regime): the lower consumer valuations are, the more firms exploit consumer information, but the lower the level of information provision. Firms even subsidise consumers if their valuations are very low or if competition intensity in the market is high enough. Firms represent bottlenecks on consumer information, and leave the data broker with zero surplus. On the other hand, if consumer valuations are sufficiently high, firms do not engage in disclosure of consumer information (high-privacy regime) and always charge positive prices.

85. If consumers can only single-home, a merger to monopoly increases market power but is privacy-neutral. When I consider consumer multi-homing, I show that firms' business strategies are altered and depend on multi-homing incentives, competition intensity, and firms' ability to monetise multi-homer information. In particular, if firms are unable to generate revenues from the information provided by multi-homers, firms charge higher prices and set lower disclosure levels compared to the case where they can monetise this information. The surplus of the data broker increases as there are more multi-homers. I find that a merger to monopoly improves the firms' ability to monetise multi-homer information. The merger decreases prices and privacy levels, and harms consumers.

Chapter 1
Merging In-Market vs Cross-Border: The Impact of Merger Policy

1. Introduction

86. There are heated debates today on mergers, particularly in network industries. In a changing economic environment impacted by liberalisation and digitalisation, firms evaluate merger opportunities not only in their domestic markets, but also across borders. In the railway industry, the French firm Alstom was willing to merge with the German firm Siemens, thereby creating the world number two leader in the industry. While the European Commission (EC) prohibited this acquisition, a central argument exposed by the merging parties was that by joining their forces, they would be able to effectively compete with the world number one leader, the chinese company CRRC. The European Commission prohibited Siemens' proposed acquisition of Alstom under the EU Merger Regulation. The main argument was that this merger would harm competition in markets for railway signalling systems and very high-speed trains. Moreover, the parties did not offer sufficient remedies to address these concerns. In an EC press release on 6 February 2019,[47] commissioner M. Vestager explained:[48]

> Millions of passengers across Europe rely every day on modern and safe trains. Siemens and Alstom are both champions in the rail industry. Without sufficient remedies, this merger would have resulted in higher prices for the signalling systems that keep passengers safe and for the next generations of very high-speed trains. The Commission prohibited the merger because the companies were not willing to address our serious competition concerns.

87. The Alstom-Siemens case[49] illustrates the trend of firms to merge cross-border and sheds light on the stakes for merger policy.[50]

---

47 Available at https://ec.europa.eu/commission/presscorner/detail/en/IP_19_881

48 According to the Financial Times on 21 January 2019, French and German officials also stepped up pressure over the Alstom-Siemens deal. French economy minister B. Lemaire said: "The German and French governments are in favour of the merger as are the heads of Siemens and Alstom. It's the best response to the rising power of the Chinese in the rail sector".https://www.ft.com/content/4bcd2b78-1d9a-11e9-b126-46fc3ad87c65

49 Note that after the failed merger between Alstom and Siemens, Alstom ultimately took over Bombardier Transport (a Canadian company). See *Les Echos, 29 January 2021*. https://www.lesechos.fr/industrie-services/tourisme-transport/alstom-prend-definitivement-les-commandes-de-bombardier-transport-1285564

50 Following the onset of COVID-19 crisis, the European Commission published a guidance document (25 March 2020) in which it advised EU Member States to strengthen their monitoring tools on foreign investments in order to protect strategic assets. This document raises the question of how (foreign)

88. In the telecommunications industry in the EU, telecommunications companies regularly question the severity of merger policy towards in-market mergers. For example, the telecommunications firms Telenor and TeliaSonera announced that they had called off plans to merge in the Danish market after they were unable to win approval from Europe's antitrust authorities. While for the European regulator, this in-market merger would have raised serious competition concerns, the firms argued that this would have created a market player with the scale and ability to compete and invest.[51] On the other hand, the EC has expressed its desire for the emergence of pan-European telecommunications firms, preferably through cross-border mergers. According to the Financial Times on 22 October 2015,[52] while regulators at the EC are turning up their noses at in-country consolidation, they have signalled that cross-border consolidation to create pan-European networks would be welcomed. Indeed, Andrus Ansip, digital commissioner, stated:

> Cross-border consolidation can be a way to integrate networks as we move towards a pan-European telecoms market. It can allow telecoms companies to expand beyond national borders and tap fully into Europe's massive customer base.

89. However, some telecoms executives were sceptical about the prospects of cross-border merging, such as Orange CEO Stéphane Richard:[53]

> Cross-border consolidation is easier but it doesn't make a lot of sense for synergies or interest.

90. This illustrates the interplay between merger policy, in-market and cross-border mergers. It is in this context that we examine how merger policy impacts the trade-off between in-market and cross-border merging.

91. An in-market merger is assessed based on a trade-off between efficiency gains and market power (Williamson, 1968). Depending on whether a merger's net impact on consumer welfare is positive or negative, an in-market merger is cleared or not, respectively, and if cleared, it can be subject to merger remedies (Farrell and Shapiro, 1990; Perry and Porter, 1985; McAfee and Williams, 1992). This differs from a cross-border merger, which is a priori less prone to issues arising from increased market power. Moreover, it does not directly affect the number of firms in either the home market or in a foreign market.

92. Therefore , if merger policy gives priority on market power issues, one could argue that it should rather focus on in-market mergers. In such a case, one could expect that it would merely impact the decision to merge in-market. However, this reasoning misses that after a failed cross-border merger, a firm may wish to exit

---

cross-border mergers should be considered due to this crisis. https://trade.ec.europa.eu/doclib/docs/2020/march/tradoc_158676.pdf

51 *New-York Times, 11 September 2015.* https://www.nytimes.com/2015/09/12/business/dealbook/telenor-teliasonera-call-off-merger.html

52 *Financial Times, 22 October 2015.* https://www.ft.com/content/ed4fc186-773a-11e5-933d-efcdc3c11c89

53 In the same way, the CEO of Telecom Italia stated that "there is no value creation" and only an "M&A play" from cross-border deals. *Financial Times, 22 October 2015.* https://www.ft.com/content/ed4fc186-773a-11e5-933d-efcdc3c11c89

by an in-market merger. Indeed, due to the presence of asymmetric information on the foreign market (Qiu and Zhou, 2006), a firm merging cross-border faces uncertainty in its post-merger profitability. If ex post the cross-border merger happens to be unprofitable, the firm would be willing to exit the foreign market.[54] This would involve having to sell its foreign subsidiary to another competitor, hence involving an in-market merger if it were sold to a firm from the foreign market. In such a case, the possibility of exiting the foreign market will rest on the leniency of merger policy (Mason and Weeds, 2013).[55] Hence, we study the trade-off between in-market and cross-border merging by focusing on the ex ante effect of merger policy on exit possibility.

93. To this end, we build a simple model with four firms competing in a regional market, which is composed of two markets: a home market and a foreign market. Such markets are segmented and of same size, with two firms in each. In the beginning, firms earn identical profits. The merger policy, set at the regional level, is defined by the probability of merging in-market. After observing the merger policy, a firm chooses between cross-border or in-market merging. Thereafter, it may decide to demerge depending on the merger outcome. It is assumed that an in-market merger is always profitable and efficient (but still subject to competitive concerns). On the other hand, a cross-border merger has a certain probability of being profitable but is initially not subject to merger policy. In fact, if the firm demerges after a cross-border merger, undoing the merger may involve an exit through an in-market merger, contingent on merger policy. In what follows, we elaborate on the results under this framework.

94. First, we determine that when no exit possibilities exist, a more lenient merger policy incentivises in-market mergers at the expense of cross-border mergers. This is explained by the merger policy only impacting the expected payoff from in-market merging; all things being equal, a firm would rather choose the in-market option. In contrast, when an exit is possible, a more lenient merger policy also impacts positively the payoff from cross-border merging. We show this to be due to lowering of exit barriers. The trade-off between both merger types is therefore altered insofar as merger policy affects the incentives for in-market and cross-border mergers differently. From a policy point of view, our results suggest that the merger policy should consider subsequent mergers triggered by an initial decision to merge. In our framework, this corresponds to the scenario of an exit-by-merger after a failed cross-border merger. Finally, our results are still

---

54 An interesting example is that of Orange and Deutsche Telekom in the UK with their foreign company EE that was sold to BT. An exit occurred for several reasons, including, as stated in Le Monde on 16 December 2014, the difficulty of identifying synergies. https://www.lemonde.fr/economie/article/2014/12/16/pourquoi-orange-quitte-le-royaume-uni-pourquoi-bt-revient-dans-les-mobiles_4541081_3234.html

55 In this respect, the Uber-Grab deal is a relevant example. In fact, Uber's exit from Southeast Asia was under scrutiny from Competition Commission of Singapore (CCS). The regulator suspected that Uber's exit-by-merger (with Grab, which is Singapore-based) could hamper competition (see https://techcrunch.com/2018/03/30/singapore-says-uber-grab-deal-may-violate-competition-laws/). Grab ultimately took over Uber's assets and operations while Uber held a 28% stake in Grab. Following the deal, the CCS observed that Grab fare prices increase by 10-15% and that Grab imposed exclusive contracts on its drivers. The CCS actually fined Uber and Grab $9.5 million for having violated Singapore's competition laws. https://techcrunch.com/2018/09/23/uber-and-grab-hit-with-9-5m-in-fines/

robust to asymmetric markets, although there is slightly less scope for cross-border compared to in-market merging.

95. This analysis focuses on the issue of exit barriers when a firm decides on a merger insofar as in some situations, the merger policy, if too restrictive, may discourage the merger. In an international context, this could affect negatively the incentives to merge cross-border when the outcome of a cross-border merger is uncertain. This analysis can therefore serve as an additional tool for a policymaker whose objective is to build a market with "global players". Indeed, our analysis suggests that a policymaker, by taking into account the trade-off between in-market and cross-border mergers, can shape a regional market consolidation.

96. Section 2 is a literature review. Section 3 describes the model framework. In Section 4, we examine the firm's decision to merge cross-border or in-market, if exit by merger is not possible. In Section 5, we determine how the possibility of exit by merger modifies the firm's merger choice. In Section 6, we provide a welfare analysis. In Section 7, we present an extension to the main model. In Section 8, the framework is discussed. Section 9 concludes. All proofs are in Appendix A.

2. Relation to Literature

97. This chapter is linked to the seminal literature on horizontal mergers. Williamson (1968) exposes the welfare trade-offs of a merger. A merger results in an increased market power, which decreases the quantity produced and increases prices, thereby inducing a dead-weight loss. On the other hand, if cost-savings from the merger are high enough, there are efficiency gains. Then, a merger will be welfare-increasing (decreasing) if the efficiency gains are higher (lower) than the dead-weight loss induced by increased market power. In a model where firms competes in quantities, Farrell and Shapiro (1990) analyse the nature and the magnitude of internal efficiencies that are required for a merger to reduce prices and increase output to the benefit of consumers. They find that for prices to decrease after a merger, the merged firm must realise a substantially lower marginal cost than did either of its constituent firms before the merger. They also find that if the internal efficiencies only consist of output rationalisation or fixed cost savings, then there will be a price increase after the merger. Then, rationalisation but not fixed cost savings, may be combined with other cost savings leading to lower prices. Traditional analysis of merger incentives can also be found in Perry and Porter (1985) and McAfee and Williams (1992), among others.

98. The chapter is also linked to the industrial organisation literature dealing with entry and merger policy. Marino and Zabojnik (2006) show that if entry is easy, and entrants exert competitive pressure on the merging firms, then merging firms will be driven in their merger decisions by a search for efficiency as opposed to being driven by motivations to increase market power. They focus

on the time dimension of entry following a merger. If new entry is relatively fast, the incumbent would not merge to increase their market power. In other words, if a merger is initiated in an industry where new entry would follow relatively quickly, the merger is more likely to generate synergies. Otherwise, it would not be attempted in the first place. Interestingly, they also show that a decrease in exogenous entry costs can increase the incumbent firms' incentives to monopolise the market through a horizontal merger. Marino and Zabojnik (2006) address the impact of entry on merger policy, whereas we focus on the impact of merger policy on entry (a cross-border merger is also as an "entry" in the foreign market).

99. Closer to our approach, Mason and Weeds (2013) explore the extent to which merger policy can act as an entry barrier. They employ a dynamic model with stochastically changing demand to assess the effects of the failing firm argument on entry and entrepreneurial activity. In their model, firms are allowed to use the failing firm defence as a (preferred) alternative to exit if they are facing poor market conditions. The authors find that, when future profitability turns out to be too low, an option to make use of the failing firm defence stimulates entry and, therefore, competition. Based on that, they derive an optimal merger policy in the form of a threshold, beyond which it is welfare increasing to approve mergers. In other words, if ex post, a more lenient merger policy may increase concentration and decrease consumer surplus, future merger prospects increase the expected value of entry.

100. Jaunaux, Lefouili and Sand-Zantman (2017) generalise the analysis of Mason and Weeds (2013). They look for the optimal merger policy focusing on mergers that are ex post anti-competitive in that they reduce consumer surplus. Relying on state dependency, they find that the competition authority should be lenient in the state of the world where the ratio between the loss in ex post consumer surplus and the gain in the entrant's expected profit induced by the merger is the lowest. They show that the optimal merger policy is driven by this ratio, whether the competition authority knows the entry cost or it only knows its distribution. Our analysis differs from the two previous studies insofar as we scrutinise a firm's incentives to merge cross-border vs in-market in the presence of merger policy.

101. This chapter contributes to the discussion on the contestable market theory that states the idea that a firm enters a market if entry and exit barriers are not too high. Baumol, Panzar and Willig (1982) exposed the entry issue by focusing on sunk costs-irreversible investments in the industry. Sunk costs create a fundamental asymmetry between incumbents and potential entrants; they represent a barrier to entry, and also a barrier to exit by committing incumbents to future price or output strategies. Entry will occur if, and only if, the present value of future profits from successful entry exceeds the sunk costs associated with entry. In our framework, a merger policy that is too severe may act as a barrier to exit.

102. This chapter is also related to the industrial organisation literature considering endogenous antitrust authorities. Nocke and Whinston (2013) explore the optimal merger policy when the antitrust authority observes the characteristics of proposed mergers but cannot observe the characteristics nor the feasibility

of mergers that are not proposed. They find that, to be approved, mergers that result in a larger computed post-merger Herfindahl index must generate larger improvements in consumer surplus. This optimal policy would then be a response to a fundamental bias in firms' proposal incentives. Indeed, they show that whenever a larger merger would create a gain that is at least as large a gain (for consumers) as a smaller merger, the larger one is proposed if both would be approved. An issue is that if both would be approved, the larger merger may be proposed even when it is worse for consumers. Then, an optimal policy therefore rejects some consumer surplus-enhancing larger mergers to induce firms to propose better smaller mergers.

103. Motta and Vasconcelos (2005) model a sequential merger formation game with endogenous efficiency gains characteris ed by scale economies. In their model, they contrast two games. In the first, the myopic antitrust authority evaluates a given merger without taking into account potential subsequent mergers. This leads the myopic antitrust authority to prohibit mergers that would be welfare beneficial once taken into account and that other mergers would follow. In the second game, the antitrust authority is forward-looking and is able to correctly anticipate the future. If efficiency gains are sufficiently large, the first merger between two firms will be authorised because the antitrust authority knows that it will be followed by a subsequent merger by the outsiders which will also be authorised because this would induce inefficient exit otherwise. In the same vein, Brito (2005) explores, by the mean of revealed preferences, how an antitrust authority may accept or reject an initial merger based on subsequent alternative mergers arising from this initial merger. The author shows that the use of revealed preferences allows the antitrust authority to set an expected upper limit on the efficiency gains obtained in a given merger (when this merger increases the firms' market power). Such limit can then be compared to the lower threshold necessary for merger approval. Then, a better understanding of the firms' incentives to merge is a way to foresee the long-term consequences of approving or rejecting a proposed merger. This chapter examines how the decision to merge cross-border or in-market may trigger subsequent mergers decisions such as an exit via a merger.

104. In the international economics literature, Haufler and Nielsen (2007) compare in-market and cross-border mergers. In a linear model of Cournot competition, the authors examine open economies where there are possible cost reductions caused by a merger. This is a three-country model where two competitors in each of two countries serve their respective home markets, and all firms jointly compete in a third (world) market. In this framework, Haufler and Nielsen develop a comparative analysis of cross-border and in-market mergers. They compare mergers from private and social perspectives and show that in-market and cross-border mergers have rather different implications: for in-market mergers, a potential conflict of interest can arise between the merging firms and a national regulator, and the national merger policy tends to be too restrictive from a global efficiency perspective. This is in contrast to profitable cross-border mergers that will be cleared by either a national or a regional regulator. They find that this laissez-faire approach is globally efficient. This chapter differs from Haufler and Nielsen (2007) in that all firms compete in the regional market, while cross-border mergers are

subject to the uncertainty of their profitability. Horn and Persson (2001) focus on cross-border versus in-market mergers in the presence of trade costs. They show that an increase in trade costs can increase the profitability of in-market compared to cross-border mergers. Our analysis differs in that we assume segmented markets (i.e. no exports); consequently, merger decisions are not impacted by trade costs.

105. Our analysis is also linked to studies examining determinants and welfare effects of cross-border mergers. Bjorvatn (2004) uses a merger model in an open economy setting to show that increased competition may increase the profitability of cross-border mergers. The reason is that economic integration may intensify the pre-merger competition in the market, thereby reducing the reservation price of the target firm. In addition, economic integration in the form of lower trade costs may reduce the post-merger business stealing effect as the outside firm chooses exports rather than greenfield investment. In an oligopoly model, Chaudhuri (2014) examines the profitability of cross-border mergers. The author shows that, under strict convexity of cost functions, cross-border mergers are more likely to occur in industries that serve multiple segmented markets rather than a single integrated market. By contrast with the previous literature on integrated markets, Chaudhuri (2014) finds that the price rises in the market where an acquisition is made whereas it falls in the other, decreasing the acquisition price of other firms. Qiu and Zhou (2006) analyse the incentives for cross-border merging in presence of asymmetric information. They develop a model of international oligopolistic competition under asymmetric information where there are n domestic firms and one foreign firm. Domestic demand is uncertain and the foreign firm suffers from information asymmetry on the domestic market. The authors show that when domestic firms are completely informed of domestic market demand, information sharing enhances the profitability of a cross-border merger (i.e. between a domestic firm and a foreign firm). Their results are also relevant for merger policy: if demand uncertainty is large and market competition is intense, cross-border mergers should be encouraged because they are privately unprofitable but socially desirable. Under the opposite conditions, these mergers should be discouraged because such mergers reduce social welfare.[56] In this chapter, we also use the information asymmetry issue of the domestic firm on the foreign market to study the interplay between merger policy, in-market and cross-border mergers.

3. Model

106. We build a model to study how merger policy affects a firm's trade-off between in-market and cross-border merging.[57]

---

56 Other relevant studies on the determinants and welfare effects of cross-border mergers can be found in Norback and Persson (2008) and Lommerud, Straume and Sorgard (2006).

57 Such mergers are assumed to be mutually exclusive. While debatable, this assumption can be realistic in that when a firm merges, it needs cash, and additional costs (coordination, etc.) could also arise. For instance, in the telecommunications market, Orange sold EE and exited the UK market to obtain more cash and to engage in acquisitions in other European countries, among other reasons.

107. ***Market characteristics***. Consider two countries, defined as "home" and "foreign" markets. Markets are segmented (i.e. we ignore the possibility of exports) and duopolistic; firms 1 and 2 compete in the home market, while firms 3 and 4 do so in the foreign market. The firms are originally symmetric, i.e. characterised by the same constant marginal cost c of production.[58] As demands (in the home and foreign markets) are also symmetric, the firms earn identical profits, $\Pi(c)$.[59]

108. Merger control is exerted on both the home and foreign markets.[60] We assume that an in-market merger is cleared with probability $\alpha \in (0,1)$, assumed exogenous.

109. ***Agents***. Among the four firms, we assume that in the beginning, only firm 1 makes a merger decision, that is, choosing between an in-market merger (IMM), a cross-border merger (CBM), or no merger at all (status quo). Any subsequent merger decisions by remaining firms would be made conditionally on firm 1 deciding on post-merger bargaining. Figure 1 represents the market structure with merger options of firm 1.

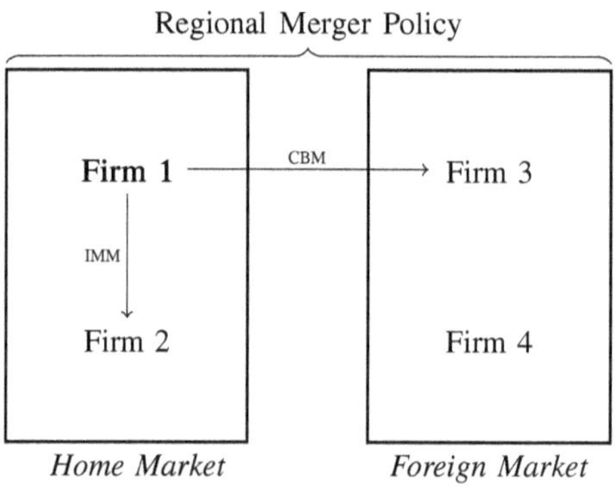

Figure 1 – Market structure

110. ***In-market merger***. Let Π_{ij} be the profit after a merger of firms i and j, with $i \neq j$. With probability α, the IMM is cleared, and the new merged entity earns a profit $\Pi_{12}(\underline{c})$ with marginal cost $\underline{c} < c$, that is, the merger leads to efficiency gains. With probability $1-\alpha$, the IMM is rejected, and firm 1 obtains its original duopoly profit $\Pi(c)$.

---

[58] The symmetric Cournot model with constant marginal costs satisfies our model assumptions. A brief Cournot version of the model is presented in Appendix B.

[59] We use a duopoly framework to simplify the analysis. This approach does not incur any serious loss of generality compared to the oligopoly case with n firms in each market.

[60] Merger policy is defined at the regional level. An example close to this idea is in the European Union, where the European Commission (EC) is in charge of merger cases with a "community dimension". An increasing convergence between national and European authorities is in fact underway (see the White Paper on merger control (EC, 2014) presented by the former VP of the EC, J. Almunia). In this respect, we abstract from conflicts between national regulators or international merger policy coordination. For more information on this, see the survey of Breinlich, Nocke and Schutz (2016).

111. ***Cross-border merger***. A CBM has an uncertain outcome. Let $\beta \in (0,1)$ be the probability that the CBM entails *market-level synergies*.[61] If firm 1 merges with firm 3, a good outcome occurs with probability β, that is, the merged entity earns a profit $\Pi_{13}(\underline{c})$ with marginal cost $\underline{c} < c$, whereas a bad outcome occurs with probability $1 - \beta$, that is, the merged entity earns a profit $\Pi_{13}(\overline{c})$ with marginal cost $\overline{c} > c$. If the CBM is efficient, efficiency gains apply to both home and foreign markets. Similarly, if the CBM is inefficient, negative spillovers apply to both markets.[62] Due to market segmentation, the CBM's profit Π_{13} is in fact the sum of profits earned separately in two countries. Finally, we assume for the sake of analysis that $\Pi_{12}(\underline{c}) \geq \Pi_{13}(\underline{c})$, that is, it is weakly more profitable to engage in an IMM than in an efficient CBM.[63]

112. In this framework, a CBM is assumed to raise no competitive concerns, because it does not affect the number of competitors and in expectation it is not price increasing (we provide the condition under which this is true in Lemma 3 of Section 5). A CBM is thus always cleared.

113. However, if there is a bad outcome after firms 1 and 3 enter into a CBM, firm 1 May decide to exit the foreign market, that is, to separate from its foreign partner, firm 3, by selling it either to firm 4 (the foreign competitor) or to firm 2 (the home competitor). Still, firm 2 would not be willing to acquire firm 3. Firm 2 in fact learns the presence of negative market-level synergies from the failed CBM, making a CBM unattractive. Therefore, an exit-by-merger can occur if firm 4 acquires firm 3 via an IMM accepted with probability α.[64] Therefore, if firm 1 finally manages to exit the foreign market, the new merged entity's profit is $\Pi_{34}(\underline{c})$; we assume firm 1 obtains its ex ante profit $\Pi(c)$ in the home market.

114. ***Payoffs***. Denote V_i^s as the expected payoff of firm i from making the merger choice $s = im, cb, e$, where *im* means in-market, *cb* denotes a cross-border merger without the possibility of exit, and *e* represents a cross-border merger with the possibility of exit. In what follows, we compare the choice of firm 1 between an IMM with firm 2 ($s = im$) or a CBM with firm 3 ($s = cb$ or e).[65]

---

61 CBMs are primarily undertaken to gain access to complementary firm-specific assets (Nocke and Yeaple, 2008), capabilities that are non-mobile across countries (Nocke and Yeaple, 2007), or country-specific assets (Norback and Persson, 2007). Therefore, an unprofitable CBM could be due to the absence of complementarity between firms' technologies, know-how or very high coordination costs. We presume that such issues have a larger chance of occurring with a CBM due to a higher degree of information asymmetry in the foreign market.

62 For instance, an unprofitable CBM can induce a negative organisational shock for the acquiring firm. This leads the management of the firm to make efforts to address these organisational issues, thereby generating coordination costs and lowering the firm's productivity in both markets.

63 This condition states that the monopoly profit in the home market is (weakly) greater than the sum of duopoly profits for the merged entity in the home and foreign markets. It can be explained by the fact that the merged entity has more market power in the former case than in the latter. Brito (2005) proposes a model of sequential mergers, where a merger that increases market power is also more likely to be profitable than an alternative merger where market power increases less.

64 Outside investors (e.g. vertical competitors) may also make offers to acquire firm 3. However, such transaction raises potential challenges, as outside investors may suffer from information asymmetry on the targeted market, undermining their ability to profitably acquire firm 3 (affected by the price of acquiring firm 3 from firm 1 and the expected efficiency of such acquisition). For simplicity, we ignore this possibility.

65 As firms are initially symmetric, it does not matter whether firm 1 enters into a CBM with firm 3 or 4.

115. As a merger is in fact an acquisition of one firm by another, we model an acquisition price, assumed to be the present value of future payoffs of the acquired firm if it had not merged.

116. ***Timing***. We consider the following sequence of events. First, the merger policy α is announced. Second, firm 1 observes α and decides whether to merge cross-border or in-market.[66] If it merges in-market, the merger is accepted with probability α. If it merges cross-border, the uncertainty of the merger's cost-efficiency is realised. Firm 1 pays the acquisition costs, and first-period payoffs are subsequently realised. Third, (*i*) if firm 1 has merged in-market, it decides whether to demerge from firm 2 and, (*ii*) if firm 1 has merged cross-border, firm 1 decides on exiting the foreign market by an in-market merger. Fourth, second-period payoffs are realised with a discount factor $\delta \in (0,1)$. We examine the subgame perfect equilibrium of this game.

4. Benchmark Case: No Possibility of Exit

117. In this section, we consider the benchmark case with no possibility of exit by merger after a CBM. We study firm 1's trade-off between the two types of mergers. In our model, merging in-market is always preferred to the status quo. The following lemma provides the condition for ensuring that firm 1 also prefers a CBM to the status quo.

118. **Lemma 1.** *Merging cross-border is preferred to the status quo if and only if* $\beta > \overline{\beta}^{ne}$, *where*

$$\overline{\beta}^{ne} = \frac{2\Pi(c) - \Pi_{13}(\overline{c})}{\Pi_{13}(\underline{c}) - \Pi_{13}(\overline{c})}.$$

119. The idea behind Lemma 1 is that firm 1 finds the option to merge cross-border profitable only if its expected probability to be profitable (β) is not too low. If this condition holds, both a CBM and an IMM are profitable for firm 1, and the firm then trades off between merging in-market and cross-border.

120. We make the following assumption to ensure that firm 1's decision is a choice between an IMM and a CBM:

121. **Assumption 1.** $\beta > \overline{\beta}^{ne}$.

122. We now study firm 1's decision between an IMM and a CBM. Consider first an IMM. As it is efficient, and there is no uncertainty as to its profitability, firm 1 has no incentive to demerge from firm 2.[67] Firm 1's expected payoff is:

$$V_1^{im} = (1+\delta)\left[\alpha(\Pi_{12}(\underline{c}) - \Pi(c)) + (1-\alpha)\Pi(c)\right]. \quad (1)$$

---

[66] One way to justify this observability would be to include a pre-merger competition phase as in Mason and Weeds (2013).

[67] As a result of timing, we do not consider the possibility that firm 1 engages in subsequent mergers after an IMM or a CBM. However, it could be shown that cross-border merging after a CBM is unattractive and that in-market merging after a profitable CBM should not be possible due to being too anti-competitive.

123. The meaning of equation (1) is as follows. With probability α, the merger is cleared, and firm 1 obtains the merger profit $\Pi_{12}(\underline{c})$ minus the price $\Pi(c)$ of acquiring firm 2. With probability $1-\alpha$, the merger is rejected, and firm 1 obtains the duopoly profit $\Pi(c)$.

124. Second, consider a CBM. Firm 1's expected payoff without an exit possibility is:

$$V_1^{cb} = (1+\delta)[\beta\Pi_{13}(\underline{c}) + (1-\beta)\Pi_{13}(\overline{c})] - (1+\delta)\Pi(c). \tag{2}$$

125. Merging cross-border is efficient with probability β and inefficient with probability $1-\beta$. The price of acquiring firm 3 is $(1+\delta)\Pi(c)$.

126. Equations (1) and (2) show that the merger policy parameter α impacts only IMM payoffs. Equation (1) implies that $\partial V_1^{im} / \partial\alpha = (1+\delta)[\Pi_{12}(\underline{c}) - 2\Pi(c)] > 0$, and therefore, a more lenient merger policy increases IMM payoffs while not impacting CBM payoffs. Thus, we can state the following proposition:

127. **Proposition 1.** *If there is no possibility of exit by merger, a more lenient merger policy, that is, a higher α, favours in-market mergers at the expense of cross-border mergers.*

128. Under Assumption 1, we obtain $V_1^{cb} - V_1^{im}|_{\alpha=0} > 0$. Furthermore, as $\beta < 1$, $V_1^{cb} - V_1^{im}|_{\alpha=1} < 0$. From Proposition 1, it follows that there is a threshold $\alpha^{ne} \in (0,1)$, such that firm 1 prefers merging in-market if $\alpha > \alpha^{ne}$ and prefers merging cross-border otherwise.

5. Possibility of Exit

129. In this section, we consider the possibility of exit by merger. As already explained, such possibility means that firm 1 would be able to sell firm 3 to the foreign company, firm 4. In this respect, we study firm 1's trade-off between both types of mergers. The following lemma provides the condition that ensures that if there is a possibility of exit, firm 1 prefers a CBM to the status quo.

130. **Lemma 2.** *If there is a possibility of exit, cross-border merging is preferred to the status quo if and only if $\delta/(1+\delta) < [\Pi_{13}(\underline{c}) - \Pi_{13}(\overline{c})]/\alpha\Pi(c)$, and $\beta > 0$.*

131. While the minimum β such that a CBM is preferred to the status quo is $\beta^{ne} > 0$ in the benchmark case (Lemma 1), we observe from Lemma 2 that this minimum β is now equal to zero. Therefore, firm 1 has more incentives to merge cross-border when it can exit by merger than when it cannot.

132. We make the following assumption to ensure that firm 1's trade-off is between an IMM and a CBM:

133. **Assumption 2.** $\delta/(1+\delta) < [\Pi_{13}(\underline{c}) - \Pi_{13}(\overline{c})]/\alpha\Pi(c)$.

134. We now examine the conditions under which an exit-by-merger can occur. Notably, if firm 1 has merged profitably cross-border with firm 3, it is better off than in the status quo and, hence, has no incentives to exit the foreign market. On the other hand, if the CBM was determined to be unprofitable, an exit may occur, in

which case it would involve firm 1 as the seller and firm 4 as the buyer. Firm 1 bargains with firm 4 through a take-it-or-leave-it offer, making firm 4 indifferent between buying firm 3 and the status quo. It therefore offers a selling price equal to $\Pi_{34}(\underline{c}) - \Pi_4(c,\overline{c})$, where $\Pi_4(c,\overline{c})$ is firm 4's profit in a scenario of firm 1 having entered into an unprofitable CBM. To ensure that exit is possible, we assume that firm 4 will accept firm 1's offer.[68]

135. IMM payoffs are the same as in the benchmark case (equation (1)). Consider firm 1's CBM payoffs if exit by merger is possible:

$$\begin{aligned} V_1^e &= \beta\Pi_{13}(\underline{c}) + (1-\beta)\Pi_{13}(\overline{c}) \\ &+ \delta[\beta\Pi_{13}(\underline{c}) + (1-\beta)(\alpha(\Pi(c) + \Pi_{34}(\underline{c}) - \Pi_4(c,\overline{c})) + (1-\alpha)\Pi_{13}(\overline{c}))] \\ &-(1+\delta)\Pi(c). \end{aligned} \quad (3)$$

136. The first line in equation (3) represents the first-period payoff (net of the acquisition price). The second line corresponds to the second-period payoff, discounted with $\delta \in (0,1)$. With probability β, firm 1 has profitably merged cross-border. With probability $1-\beta$, it has not profitably merged cross-border and decides to exit the foreign market via a merger. With probability α, firm 4 acquires firm 3, and firm 1 obtains its ex ante profit $\Pi(c)$ plus the selling price $\Pi_{34}(\underline{c}) - \Pi_4(c,\overline{c})$. With probability $1-\alpha$, the IMM between firms 3 and 4 is rejected, and firm 1 obtains the profit $\Pi_{13}(\overline{c})$. The third line corresponds to the CBM acquisition price. Let $\Delta E = \Pi(c) + \Pi_{34}(\underline{c}) - \Pi_4(c,\overline{c}) - \Pi_{13}(\overline{c}) > 0$ be firm 1's exit payoff.[69] The payoff from cross-border merging can be simplified to:

$$V_1^e = V_1^{cb} + \delta\alpha(1-\beta)\Delta E. \quad (4)$$

137. The merger policy α now impacts both IMM and CBM payoffs. Indeed, we obtain:

$$\frac{\partial V_1^{im}}{\partial \alpha} = (1+\delta)[\Pi_{12}(\underline{c}) - 2\Pi(c)] > 0; \quad (5)$$

$$\frac{\partial V_1^e}{\partial \alpha} = \delta(1-\beta)\Delta E > 0. \quad (6)$$

138. From equations (5 and 6), we observe that in addition to increasing IMM payoffs, the merger policy now positively affects CBM payoffs. The intuition is that a more lenient merger policy increases the profitability of exit by merger after an unprofitable CBM. Therefore, there are lower barriers to exit. An additional insight obtained from (6) is that if the probability of a profitable

68 At the other extreme, we could assume that it is firm 4 that makes a take-it-or-leave-it offer to firm 1. Firm 4 would then set a price for firm 3 making firm 1 indifferent between staying in the foreign market and exiting the foreign market by selling firm 3. Firm 4 would thus offer a purchase price equal to $\Pi_{13}(\overline{c}) - \Pi(c)$. In this case, the merger policy α has no effect on the payoff from cross-border merging, V_1^e. A more general case would imply a bargaining power that is not fully in the hands of firm 1 or firm 4; in such an intermediate case, the merger policy would affect payoff from cross-border merging, V_1^e.

69 In a linear Cournot setting, ΔE is positive, except in the case where the IMM yields almost zero efficiency gains, while the CBM is extremely unprofitable.

CBM decreases (i.e. β is lower), the positive effect of merger policy is more significant ($\partial^2 V_1^e / \partial\alpha\partial\beta = -\delta\Pi(c) < 0$). Hence, we can state the following proposition:

139. **Proposition 2.** *When an exit-by-merger is possible, a more lenient merger policy, that is, a higher α,positively impacts the incentives to merge cross-border by lowering the exit barriers.*

140. We now study the impact of merger policy on the decision to merge cross-border versus in-market. We compare the effects of merger policy and observe that:

$$\frac{\partial\left[V_1^e - V_1^{im}\right]}{\partial\alpha} \leq 0 \quad \text{if} \quad \frac{\delta}{1+\delta} \leq \frac{\Pi_{12}(\underline{c}) - 2\Pi(c)}{(1-\beta)\Delta E}; \tag{7}$$

$$\frac{\partial\left[V_1^e - V_1^{im}\right]}{\partial\alpha} > 0 \quad \text{otherwise.} \tag{8}$$

141. Equation (7) means that merger policy has a stronger effect on the decision to merge in-market than to merge cross-border, while equation (8) states the contrary. From equations (5 and 6), merger policy impacts the entire gain from merging in-market while impacting only the second-period CBM payoff if firm 1 exits by merger. Hence, we assume that equation (7) holds for the rest of the analysis.

142. We can now analyse how the trade-off between both merger types is altered compared to the benchmark case. Under Assumption 1, we obtain $V_1^e - V_1^{im}\,|_{\alpha=0} > 0$. Furthermore, for $\delta/(1+\delta) < [\Pi_{12}(\underline{c}) - (\beta\Pi_{13}(\underline{c}) + (1-\beta)\Pi_{13}(\overline{c}))]/(1-\beta)\Delta E$, $V_1^e - V_1^{im}\,|_{\alpha=1} < 0$. Hence, it follows that there is a threshold $\alpha^e \in (0,1)$, such that firm 1 prefers in-market merging if $\alpha > \alpha^e$ and prefers cross-border merging otherwise. Comparing thresholds α^{ne} and α^e, we state the following proposition:

143. **Proposition 3.** *Cross-border merging is preferred to in-market merging for higher values of α, that is, $\alpha^e > \alpha^{ne}$.*

144. Proposition 3 states that if an exit-by-merger is possible, there is more scope for cross-border merging. Figure 2 illustrates this idea. In the figure, we observe that as α increases, firm 1 is more inclined to merge in-market than cross-border in all cases. Nonetheless, when an exit-by-merger is possible, firm 1 merges cross-border rather than in-market for a larger range of values of α, since $\alpha^e > \alpha^{ne}$. This occurs because merger policy now directly affects the CBM decision. If α is very high, firm 1 will always opt for an IMM, whereas if α is very low, firm 1 will always opt for a CBM. If α is between α^{ne} and α^e, the firm chooses an IMM when exit is not possible and a CBM if exit-by-merger is possible.

145. Finally, another interesting insight is that with exit-by-merger, a stricter merger policy, that is, a lower α, now makes both IMM and CBM less profitable in expectation, contrary to what has been determined in the benchmark case. If the merger policy is quite severe (very low α) and the expected profitability from merging cross-border is low (small β), a status quo may be preferred to any merger. Therefore, while the severity of merger policy would prevent those mergers that are possibly anti-competitive, this may also discourage potentially pro-competitive mergers, such as cross-border mergers.

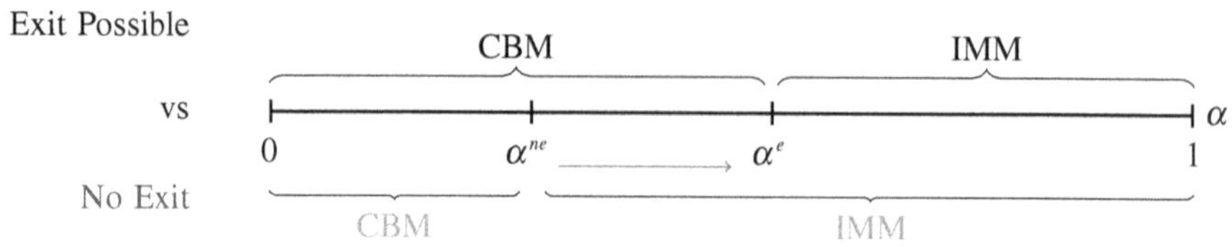

Figure 2 – Merger decision: with vs without a possible exit

6. Welfare Analysis

146. In this section, we apply basic comparative statics to examine the impact of firm 1's merger choice on social welfare, defined as the sum of firms' profits and consumer surplus in both markets. Denote $W(\alpha)$ as the (expected) social welfare function.

147. Let $p(c,c)$ denote the status quo price, $p(\underline{c},c)$ denote the price after a profitable CBM, and $p(\overline{c},c)$ denote the price after an unprofitable CBM. We use the following lemma to ensure that a CBM is in expectation never price-increasing:[70]

148. **Lemma 3.** *In expectation, a CBM is never price-increasing if*

$$\beta \geq \beta_p \equiv \frac{p(c,c) - p(\overline{c},c)}{p(\underline{c},c) - p(\overline{c},c)}.$$

149. We make the following assumption:

150. **Assumption 3.** $\beta \geq \beta_p$.

151. In the benchmark case, an exit-by-merger is not possible, and merger policy only affects IMMs. If firm 1 merges in-market, the merger is either welfare-increasing or decreasing, and $W(\alpha)$ is monotonic on $\left[\alpha^{ne},1\right)$. If firm 1 merges cross-border, $W(\alpha)$ does not depend on α. This means that for $\alpha \in \left(0,\alpha^{ne}\right)$, $W(\alpha) = W^{cb}$, where the constant W^{cb} is the welfare level if an exit-by-merger is not possible.

152. When an exit-by-merger is possible, the merger policy also affects CBMs. If firm 1 merges in-market, $W(\alpha)$ is monotonic on $\left[\alpha^{e},1\right)$. If firm 1 merges cross-border, $W(\alpha)$ now depends on α and is monotonic on $\left(0,\alpha^{e}\right)$. Indeed, if an exit-by-merger occurs, it will be either welfare-increasing or decreasing.[71] We therefore state the following proposition:

153. **Proposition 4.** *In the benchmark case, if $\alpha < \alpha^{ne}$, social welfare does not depend on α and a cross-border merger always has a positive impact on social welfare ($\beta \geq \beta_p$). If an exit-by-merger is possible, if $\alpha < \alpha^{e}$, social welfare depends on α and a cross-border merger decreases (increases) social welfare if the exit-by-merger is welfare-decreasing (increasing).*

---

70 Therefore, we focus only on the welfare impact of an exit-by-merger due to an unprofitable CBM.

71 Mathematical details on welfare levels can be found in Appendix A.

154. Figure 3 shows an example of differences between the benchmark case and that of a possible exit. Let $W(1^-)$ be the limit of $W(\alpha)$ when α goes to 1^- and $W(\alpha^{e-})$ be the limit of $W(\alpha)$ when α goes to α^{e-}. On the left graph (the benchmark case), a CBM occurs if $(0,\alpha^{ne})$ and $W(\alpha)=W^{cb}$, whereas an IMM occurs if $[\alpha^{ne},1)$ and is welfare-increasing. As α increases and approaches 1, social welfare becomes higher under an IMM (e.g. $W^{cb} < W(1^-)$). However, on the right graph (an exit is possible), a CBM occurs if $(0,\alpha^{e})$ and is welfare-increasing in such scenario. As α increases and approaches α^{e}, social welfare increases under a CBM (e.g. $W(\alpha^{e-}) > W(1^-)$). Therefore, a corollary from Proposition welfare CBM is that considering the possibility of an exit, we are better able to determine whether a CBM, an IMM, or no merger is most beneficial to social welfare.

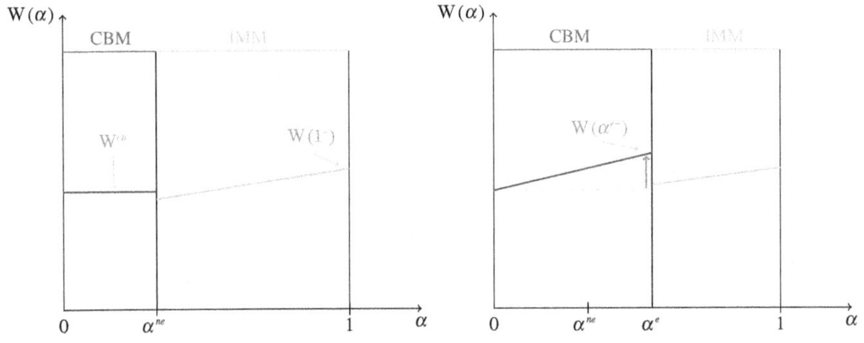

Figure 3 – Welfare: the benchmark scenario (left) vs that of a possible exit (right)

7. Asymmetric Markets

155. In this section, we assume asymmetric markets, with the home market being a duopoly, and the foreign market being an oligopoly of $n > 2$ firms.

156. Let us study the incentives for firm 1 to merge cross-border and in-market, as a function of the number of firms in the foreign market. If firm 1 merges in-market, its profits are unchanged, as the IMM benefits are independent of the foreign market structure. Thus, the incentives for IMMs are unchanged. On the contrary, when firm 1 merges cross-border, its profits are $\Pi_{13}(\underline{c}) = \Pi_1(\underline{c},2) + \Pi_3(\underline{c},n)$ with probability β and $\Pi_{13}(\overline{c}) = \Pi_1(\overline{c},2) + \Pi_3(\overline{c},n)$ with probability $1-\beta$ (where the second term in parentheses designates the number of firms in the market). As the foreign market is now less concentrated, CBM profits are lower than in the baseline model. In this case and independently from the merger policy, cross-border merging is less beneficial. Then, suppose that for β that is not too low, $V_1^{cb}(n) < V_1^{cb}$ and $V_1^{e}(n) < V_1^{e}$, and let $\alpha^{ne}(n)$ and $\alpha^{e}(n)$ designate the

threshold values of α for asymmetric markets.[72] We can state the following proposition:

157. **Proposition 5.** *With $n > 2$ firms on the foreign market, there is slightly less scope for cross-border merging compared to in-market merging, that is, $\alpha^{ne}(n) < \alpha^{ne}$, and $\alpha^{e}(n) < \alpha^{e}$.*

158. Considering welfare, our analysis is the same as in the previous section, except that (i) the mergers' thresholds are changed, and (ii) an exit-by-merger is more likely to be welfare-increasing, as the foreign market is less concentrated. Therefore, despite the fact that CBMs appear less attractive, our conclusions regarding the trade-off between IMM and CBM still hold.

8. Discussion

159. In this section, we review some elements of our framework and suggest future research directions.

160. In our framework, the home and foreign markets are concentrated *ex ante*. In practice, a competition authority would thus expect efficiency gains sufficiently high to compensate for the potential anti-competitive effects of the merger. This may entail merger remedies.[73] Introducing merger remedies in our framework would affect the trade-off between an IMM and a CBM. Two types of merger remedies can be contemplated: structural remedies (e.g. allowing entry of a new market player) or behavioral ones (e.g. a price cap). Such remedies would have two main effects on merger prospects. On the one hand, merger remedies would mitigate potential anti-competitive effects, thereby increasing the probability of merger acceptance α for an IMM. On the other hand, the profitability of an in-market merger would be reduced, due to lower gains in market power. The former effect will tend to encourage the choice to merge in-market rather than cross-border. The latter effect will rather favour cross-market mergers.[74] In sum, we expect that merger remedies will impact the trade-off between an IMM and a CBM in an ambiguous way.

161. Moreover, in this framework we do not consider the presence of a potential outsider, neither in the home market nor in the foreign one. If we relax this assumption, a merger-to-monopoly in the home market may induce entry of an outside firm in the same market, provided that entry barriers are not too high. The post-merger entry of an outsider has the same (ambiguous) effect on the trade-off between an IMM and a CBM than (structural) merger remedies: on the one hand,

72 A value of β that is not too low ensures the validity of assumptions on $V_1^s(n)$ and V_1^s.

73 For an analysis along these lines, see Chone and Linnemer (2008) and Dertwinkel-Kalt and Wey (2016).

74 An example is the aborted merger project between TeliaSonera and Telenor in Denmark (2016). To clear the merger, the European Commission required a structural merger remedy, i.e. the entry of new firm. Therefore, the merging firms cancelled their merger project (*Les Echos, 12 May 2016*). https://www.lesechos.fr/2016/05/coup-de-froid-sur-les-operations-nationales-228314.

it increases the probability that the competition authority clears the IM merger, favoring IMM over CBM; on the other hand, it decreases the profitability of an IM merger, leading the firm to favour CBM over IMM.

162. Finally, alternative scenarios could be explored. For instance, in a framework where in-market merging has an uncertain outcome, one aim of merger policy could be to protect local consumers from unprofitable IMMs. One way to do so would be to encourage CBMs that generate market level synergies (e.g. know-how). However, if due to the severity of merger policy, exit barriers were higher, firms may be deterred from merging cross-border and local consumers may be damaged. Moreover, in the scenario where an IMM is found to be unprofitable, an exit by the mean of a cross-border merger may be considered, i.e. a domestic firm selling its domestic subsidiary to a foreign firm. In this case, exit prospects will depend on expected market level synergies of cross-border merging. The analysis of these scenarios is left to future research.

9. Conclusion

163. This chapter examines how merger policy impacts the trade-off between in-market and cross-border mergers. We first study a benchmark case where an exit-by-merger is impossible and hence that merger policy only affects in-market merger's profitability. We find that a stricter (more lenient) merger policy shifts firms' decisions towards cross-border mergers (in-market mergers). On the contrary, if it is possible to exit by merger, we find that the merger policy also affects the incentives to merge cross-border by lowering (or increasing) exit barriers. The trade-off between both merger types is therefore altered, as the merger policy affects the incentives to merge in-market and cross-border differently. In this respect, we determine the thresholds values for which a firm chooses an IMM when exit is not possible while it chooses a CBM if exit-by-merger is possible. Our analysis then implies that if the merger policy were very strict and market-level synergies were low (i.e. the payoff from merging would be low), firms would ultimately not merge at all. Examining welfare, we find that if the possibility of exit is considered, the merger policy affects cross-border in addition to in-market mergers because a CBM may induce a subsequent merger (exit-by-merger). This suggests that a policy maker is therefore better able to determine whether a CBM, an IMM, or no merger at all is the most relevant scenario to social welfare.

164. The framework presented in this chapter is specific and relies on a number of assumptions. We used a simple reduced-form model, which does not incorporate all the dimensions at play in mergers and in merger assessment. Using this specific model, we show that merger policy affects firms' trade-off between in-market and cross-border mergers. A more general model would enable the qualification of these results, for example by providing a more detailed model of the merger assessment process by a competition authority. This is left to future research.

Appendix A

Definition of α^{ne}

165. Under Assumption 1, we have $V_1^{cb} - V_1^{im}|_{\alpha=0} > 0$. Furthermore, $V_1^{cb} - V_1^{im}|_{\alpha=1} < 0$ if $\beta < (\Pi_{12}(\underline{c}) - \Pi_{13}(\overline{c})) / (\Pi_{13}(\underline{c}) - \Pi_{13}(\overline{c}))$. Since $\Pi_{12}(\underline{c}) \geq \Pi_{13}(\underline{c})$, this inequality holds if $\beta < 1$.

Proof of Lemma 2

166. Firm 1 prefers cross-border merging to the status quo if $V_1^e \geq (1+\delta)\Pi(c)$, or if

$$\beta\underbrace{[(1+\delta)(\Pi_{13}(\underline{c}) - \Pi_{13}(\overline{c})) - \delta\alpha\Pi(c)]}_{A} \geq \underbrace{-[(1+\delta)\Pi_{13}(\overline{c}) + \delta\alpha\Pi(c)]}_{B}.$$

167. While B is negative, A is either positive or negative. First, consider if $A > 0$. We have $A > 0 \Leftrightarrow \delta/(1+\delta) < (\Pi_{13}(\underline{c}) - \Pi_{13}(\overline{c})) / \alpha\Pi(c)$, which means that $\beta \geq B/A$ where B/A is negative. In our setting, it means that the minimum β for which a CBM is preferred to the status quo is zero. Therefore, if $\delta/(1+\delta) < (\Pi_{13}(\underline{c}) - \Pi_{13}(\overline{c})) / \alpha\Pi(c)$ and $\beta > 0$, a CBM is preferred to the status quo.

168. Consider if $A < 0$. We have $A < 0 \Leftrightarrow \delta/(1+\delta) > (\Pi_{13}(\underline{c}) - \Pi_{13}(\overline{c})) / \alpha\Pi(c)$, which means that $\beta \leq B/A$ where B/A is positive. However, β being the probability of market level synergies, this case has no economic sense and is not considered.

Definition of α^e and proof of Proposition 3

169. Under Assumption 1, $V_1^{cb} - V_1^{im}|_{\alpha=0} > 0$.

$$V_1^e - V_1^{im}|_{\alpha=1} < 0 \text{ if } \delta/(1+\delta) < [\Pi_{12}(\underline{c}) - (\beta\Pi_{13}(\underline{c}) + (1-\beta)\Pi_{13}(\overline{c}))] / (1-\beta)\Delta E.$$

170. The numerator is positive as $\beta < 1$.

171. We show that $\alpha^e > \alpha^{ne}$. To this end, we compute the difference between cross-border and in-market merging payoffs with and without a possible exit.

$$\left[V_1^e(\alpha^e) - V^{im}(\alpha^e)\right] - \left[V_1^{cb} - V^{im}(\alpha^{ne})\right] = 0$$

$$\Leftrightarrow \delta\alpha^e(1-\beta)\Delta E + (1+\delta)(\alpha^{ne} - \alpha^e)[\Pi_{12}(\underline{c}) - 2\Pi(c)] = 0$$

$$\Leftrightarrow \alpha^e(\delta(1-\beta)\Delta E - (1+\delta)[\Pi_{12}(\underline{c}) - 2\Pi(c)]) + (1+\delta)\alpha^{ne}[\Pi_{12}(\underline{c}) - 2\Pi(c)] = 0$$

$$\Leftrightarrow \alpha^e = \frac{-(1+\delta)[\Pi_{12}(\underline{c}) - 2\Pi(c)]\alpha^{ne}}{\delta(1-\beta)\Delta E - (1+\delta)[\Pi_{12}(\underline{c}) - 2\Pi(c)]}.$$

172. The numerator is negative and the denominator is also negative (by equation (7)). Therefore, $\alpha^e = k\alpha^{ne}$, where

$$k \equiv \frac{-(1+\delta)[\Pi_{12}(\underline{c}) - 2\Pi(c)]}{\delta(1-\beta)\Delta E - (1+\delta)[\Pi_{12}(\underline{c}) - 2\Pi(c)]} > 1.$$

173. Therefore, $\alpha^e > \alpha^{ne}$.

Proof of Lemma 3

174. In expectation, a CBM is not price-increasing if

$$\beta p(\underline{c},c) + (1-\beta)p(\overline{c},c) \leq p(c,c)$$

$$\Leftrightarrow \beta \geq \frac{p(c,c) - p(\overline{c},c)}{p(\underline{c},c) - p(\overline{c},c)} \equiv \beta_p.$$

Detailed welfare expressions

175. If firm 1 merges in-market, the expected welfare is as follows:

$$W^{im}(\alpha) = (1+\delta)(\alpha w(\underline{c}) + (1-\alpha)w(c,c)),$$

where $w(.,.)$ is the sum of producer and consumer surpluses, which depend on marginal costs.

176. If firm 1 merges cross-border, the expected welfare is:

$$W^{cb} = (1+\delta)(\beta(w(\underline{c},c)) + (1-\beta)w(\overline{c},c)),$$

$$W^e(\alpha) = W^{cb} + \delta\alpha\left(w^e - w(c,\overline{c})\right),$$

for the benchmark case (*cb*) and with a possibility of exit (*e*), respectively, where $w^e = w(c,c) + w(\underline{c})$ is the level of social welfare after an exit via a merger.

177. Therefore, we have $W\left(1^-\right) = W^{im}\left(1^-\right) = (1+\delta)w(\underline{c})$ and $W\left(\alpha^{e-}\right) = W^e\left(\alpha^{e-}\right) = W^{cb} + \delta\alpha^{e-}\left(w^e - w(c,\overline{c})\right)$.

Proof of Proposition 5

178. We build the thresholds $\alpha^{ne}(n)$ and $\alpha^e(n)$ in the same way as in the baseline model. Given that:

$$\begin{cases} \left|V_1^{cb}(n) - V_1^{im}\right|_{|\alpha=0} < \left|V_1^{cb} - V_1^{im}\right|_{|\alpha=0}, \\ \left|V_1^{cb}(n) - V_1^{im}\right|_{|\alpha=1} > \left|V_1^{cb} - V_1^{im}\right|_{|\alpha=1}, \end{cases}$$

we deduce that $\alpha^{ne}(n) < \alpha^{ne}$. We proceed in a similar way if exit is possible to show that $\alpha^e(n) < \alpha^e$.

Appendix B

Cournot example

179. Our model assumptions are satisfied for the symmetric Cournot model.

180. Let $D(p) = a - bp$ be the monopoly demand and $D(p_i, p_j) = a - b(p_i + p_j)$ be the duopoly demand. The monopoly maximises its profit $(p - \underline{c})D(p)$ with respect to price p, whereas in a duopoly, firm i maximises its profit $(p_i - c)D(p_i, p_j)$ with respect to p_i, taking p_j as given.

181. The equilibrium profits in the different scenarios (initial duopoly game, profits after an IMM and a CBM, profitable or unprofitable) are as follows:

$$\Pi(c) = \frac{(a-c)^2}{9b},\ \Pi_{12}(\underline{c}) = \frac{(a-\underline{c})^2}{4b},\ \Pi_{13}(\underline{c}) = \frac{2(a-2\underline{c}+c)^2}{9b},\ \Pi_{13}(\overline{c}) = \frac{2(a-2\overline{c}+c)^2}{9b},$$

where we assume that $a > 2\overline{c} - c$. Note that Π_{34}, the IMM profit after an exit-by-merger, is equal to Π_{12}.

182. From Lemma 1, the minimum β such that a CBM is preferred to the status quo is:

$$\beta^{ne} = \frac{(a-\overline{c})(\overline{c}-\underline{c})}{(a+c-\overline{c}-\underline{c})(\overline{c}-c)}.$$

183. From Lemma 3, the minimum β such that, in expectation, a CBM is never price-increasing is

$$\beta_p = \frac{\overline{c}-c}{\overline{c}-\underline{c}},$$

where $\beta_p > \beta^{ne}$, meaning that in the Cournot framework, the minimum β such that a CBM is never price-increasing is higher than the minimum β making the CBM preferable to status quo.

184. **Numerical example.** As an illustration, let $a = b = 1$, $c = 0.5$, $\overline{c} = 0.6$, $\underline{c} = 0.35$, $\beta = 0.5$, and $\delta = 0.5$. In this case, $\beta^{ne} = 0.29$, $\beta_p = 0.4$, the exit payoff is "$E = 0.07$ and $\alpha^{ne} \approx 0.51 < \alpha^{e} \approx 0.7$.

185. The figure below illustrates the trade-off between in-market and cross-border merger in this numerical example for the Cournot setting.

186. If the IMM yields very limited efficiencies and the CBM is highly unprofitable, the exit payoff can be negative (as mentionned in footnote 17): for example, if $\overline{c} = 0.88$ and $\underline{c} = 0.49$, then "$E = -0.008$.

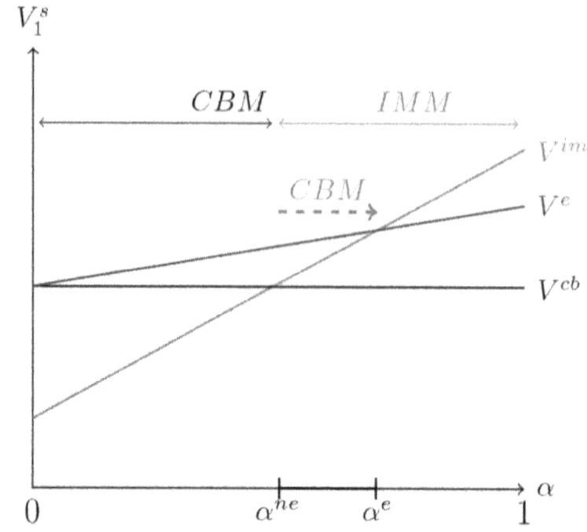

Figure 4 – IMM vs CBM trade-off – Cournot example

Chapter 2
Public vs Private Investments in Network Industries

1. Introduction

187. Due to the high costs of rolling out infrastructures, public authorities often play a key role in the deployment of new networks. In the telecommunications sector, for example, public authorities of many countries are involved in the deployment of the so-called "next-generation networks", capable of delivering high-speed access to the internet.

188. In Australia, the National Broadband Network is a nation-wide publicly funded infrastructure project, using the fibre-to-the-home (FTTH) technology, which aims to cover 93% of Australian households and businesses.[75] In the United States, the Trump administration explored the possibility of building a national 5G mobile network. Private operators and the Federal Communication Commission (FCC) raised concerns about this idea arguing that the market is the best placed to foster innovation and investment. FCC Chairman Ajit Pai stated:[76]

> I oppose any proposal for the federal government to build and operate a nationwide 5G network. The main lesson to draw from the wireless sector's development over the past three decades is that the market, not government, is best positioned to drive innovation and investment .... Any federal effort to construct a nationalised 5G network would be a costly and counterproductive distraction from the policies we need to help the United States win the 5G future.

189. Local authorities are also engaged in the roll-out of high-speed broadband infrastructures. For example, the city of Chattanooga was the first to offer 1GB/s high-speed internet access in the United States through a local public company (Electric Power Board).[77] In Europe, the province of Siena (Terrecablate) in Italy, the city of Nuenen (OnsNet) in the Netherlands, and many localities in France, among others, have invested in next-generation access infrastructures (see the roll-out for France in Figure 1).[78]

---

[75] Similarly, in New-Zealand, the Ultra-Fast Broadband Initiative is a public-private partnership of the government with four private companies, aiming at building a fibre-to-the-home network infrastructure covering 87% of the population by the end of 2022.

[76] FTC release (29/01/2018). https://apps.fcc.gov/edocs_public/attachmatch/DOC-348903A1.pdf.

[77] Other American cities have deployed public-owned fibre-optic networks offering high-speed Internet acces, e.g. Lafayette, La., Bristol, Va., etc. See *New-York Times, 4 January 2014.* https://www.nytimes.com/2014/02/04/technology/fast-internet-service-speeds-business-development-in-chattanooga.html

[78] These broadband plans are developed in accordance with the Services of General Economic Interest (SGEI) principle. SGEI are economic activities that public authorities identify as being of particular importance to

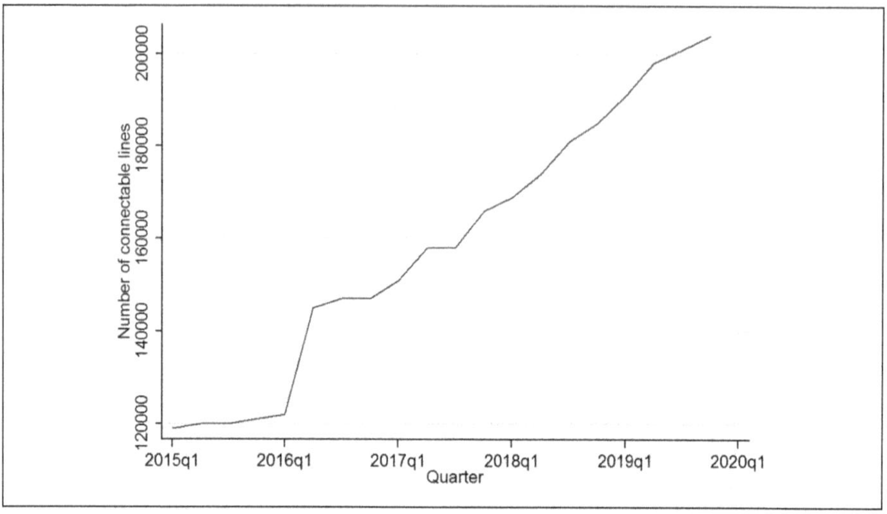

Figure 1 – Roll-out of public broadband infrastructure in France (data from ARCEP, vertically integrated public operators)

190. Public intervention in the deployment of network infrastructures is justified by a perceived market failure: because they do not internalise all the external effects from high-speed network infrastructures, the argument goes, private operators underinvest, or do not invest fast enough, compared to what would be socially desirable.

191. However, public investment in next-generation access networks is realised at the same time as private investment in other areas, but also sometimes the same areas. This has raised a hot debate on whether public investment rather crowds in or rather crowds out private investment. With the concern that public investment could undermine private investment, 20 states in the United States have passed legislation banning or restricting public provision of internet access as of 2016.[79] Tennessee state law has prevented the Electric Power Board of Chattanooga from expanding to adjacent communities that lack fast, cheap internet access.[80] Private operators also question the role of public investment. For example, AT&T wrote to the FCC that municipal broadband can bring private internet service providers (ISPs) to "operate at a competitive disadvantage", and that there should be restrictions on public broadband projects to ensure a "level playing field".[81]

192. A key issue is therefore to ensure a fair competitive environment for private firms. The Broadband Guidelines in the European Union (European Commission, 2009)

citizens and that would not be supplied (or would be supplied under different conditions) if there were no public intervention.

79 FCC 16-148. https://docs.fcc.gov/public/attachments/FCC-16-148A1.pdf.

80 Chattanooga petitioned the FCC to preempt that state law, and the FCC granted the request, using its authority to promote competition in local markets by removing barriers to infrastructure investment. However, the State of Tennessee sued the FCC to overturn its decision. The case is in process.

81 See *ARS Technica, 4 February 2016.* https://arstechnica.com/tech-policy/2016/02/att-is-the-villain-in-city-broadband-fight-republican-lawmaker-says/.

follow this objective. Public authorities face a complex trade-off here. On the one hand, there is the risk that public investment crowds out private investment, as discussed above. On the other hand, in some areas private investment will not materialise, at least in the short or medium term, due to high costs of infrastructure deployment. In this chapter, we provide a theoretical framework to study this trade-off, and characterise the potential benefits and costs of public intervention in the deployment of network infrastructures, when private firms also invest in infrastructures.

193. We build a model where a private firm competes with public firms in prices and coverage of a new network infrastructure in a given country. Firms decide simultaneously on prices for their services, and on coverage of the country with the new network. The private firm is a profit maximiser, whereas public firms maximise the sum of their profits and consumer surplus, subject to a budget constraint. We consider two scenarios of public intervention: with a national public firm and with local public firms. The national public firm charges the same uniform price all over the country, subject to a global budget constraint. Each local public firm is based in a given area of the country, and charges a price for the service that applies only locally, subject to a local budget constraint. We assume that the private firm charges a uniform price all over the country, as does the national public firm. All the areas of the country have the same demand, but the investment cost increases (at an increasing rate) as the operators turn to outlying areas.

194. First, we examine firms' decisions in a monopoly benchmark. We find that the private firm charges the monopoly price and covers up to a monopoly area where the marginal cost of investment is equal to the (local) monopoly profit. The national public firm charges a price lower than the monopoly price, and cross-subsidises between low-cost and high-cost areas. Cross-subsidies allow the national public firm to cover a larger share of the country than the private firm, up to the area where the marginal social benefit of investment becomes lower than the marginal cost of investment. Local public firms charge prices that are contingent on the investment cost in their area. They cover the same territory as the private monopoly. Total welfare is always higher with a national public firm or local public firms, compared to a private monopoly. In a specific Shubik-Levitan linear demand model, we also show that welfare is higher with a national public firm than with local public firms.

195. We then examine firms' decisions in a mixed duopoly framework, when the private firm competes with the national public firm or local public firms in prices and coverage. We focus on the case where public firms lead in investment, that is, invest more than the private firm in equilibrium. In this situation, the private firm competes with the public firms in low-cost areas, while public firms operate as a monopoly in the costlier areas.

196. When the private firm competes with the national public firm, we find that the private firm reacts to price increase of its rival by increasing its own price (strategic complementarity), whereas the national public firm reacts by decreasing its own price (strategic substituability). A larger overlap between the private firm's and the public firm's networks drives firms' prices up. The reason is that the competition from the private firm makes it harder for the public firm to break even by setting low prices. Since a larger overlap means more competition, the public firm has to

increase its price to satisfy its budget constraint. The private firm then reacts by increasing its price. In the equilibrium of the coverage-price game, we find that total coverage by the national public firm is lower than in the benchmark. Whereas competition leads the private firm to set lower prices than in the benchmark, the public firm may charge higher prices than in the benchmark. This is because the competition from the private firm makes it harder to sustain low prices.

197. When the private firm competes with local public firms, we find that a larger overlap between the private firm's network and the local public firms' networks leads to a higher price by the private firm and lower prices by the local public firms. This is because, when the private firm covers a larger territory, with more overlap with the public firms, it faces local public firms that are less aggressive in prices, as they have to charge a higher price to cover their higher investment costs. The private firm reacts to the (on average) softer competition by increasing its uniform price. Since the private firm increases its price, budget constraints of local public firms are relaxed and they then react by decreasing their own prices. In the equilibrium of the coverage-price game, total coverage is the same as in the benchmark. The private firm sets a lower price than in the benchmark, while the local public firms set higher prices.

198. Section 2 of this chapter, we discuss the related literature. Section 3 presents the model framework. In Section 4, we solve the model in a monopoly benchmark. We study the mixed duopoly between a private firm and a national public firm in Section 5, and the mixed duopoly between the private firm and local public firms in Section 6. Section 7 concludes.

2. Related Literature

199. This chapter is related to three strands of literature on (i) the impact of regulation on the roll-out of network infrastructures, (ii) mixed oligopolies, and (iii) public intervention for investment in new networks.

200. In the first strand of literature, various studies have analysed the impact of universal service obligations (USOs) on the deployment of network infrastructures. Valletti, Hoernig and Barros (2002) examine the impact of universal service obligations as a form of regulation that puts constraints on firms' pricing and coverage decisions. Uniform pricing constraints oblige firms to offer their services at a geographically uniform price, whereas coverage constraints oblige firms to cover at least a given area. The authors show that the entrant's coverage and total coverage can be smaller with the uniform pricing constraint than without it. They also show that there are trade-offs between larger coverage and higher welfare of served consumers, and between consumer welfare in markets with competition or monopoly. With the uniform pricing constraint, the benefits of competition, in terms of lower prices, are distributed to all consumers, even those not served by the entrant. On the other hand, in duopoly areas consumers are charged a higher price and firms' coverage levels are lower. If the regulator imposes a high coverage constraint, the number of consumers increases, but consumers in low-cost areas are hurt by higher prices.

This is because larger coverage softens competition: the incumbent is less willing to compete for market share and is thus more accommodating.

201. Similar results on the impact of uniform pricing constraints have been obtained by Anton, Vander Weide and Vettas (2002), Chone, Flochel and Perrot (2000, 2002) and Foros and Kind (2003). Hoernig (2006) shows that the opening of the market to competition in the presence of uniform pricing constraints on all operators – both incumbent and entrant operators – gives rise to a series of neighbouring monopolies rather than competition for customers. In a more general framework, Gautier and Wauthy (2010) show that under uniform pricing obligations, the incumbent has conflicting incentives: on one hand, it may be tempted to "withdraw" to regions with limited competition and charge high prices, leaving the more competitive regions to the entrant; alternatively, it may be willing to undercut the entrant to win market share. Gautier and Wauthy show that, because of this conflict, an equilibrium in pure-strategies may fail to exist.

202. This chapter is also related to the literature on access regimes and investment incentives. Some papers examine the impact of access on the investment incentives of incumbent operators (Foros (2004) and Nitsche and Wiethaus (2011)), while other papers analyze entrants' investment incentives (Bourreau and Doğan, 2006). Bourreau, Cambini and Hoernig (2015) investigate the impact of different access regimes on investment in different geographical areas of a country. Two different access regimes are studied. In the "duplication-based" regulatory regime, the regulator sets different access prices in areas with a single infrastructure and in areas with multiple competing infrastructures. In the "competition-based" regulatory regime, the regulator sets the access price only in areas where just one infrastructure is present, and leaves it to the market when multiple infrastructures are present, expecting competition to arise at the wholesale level. Their main finding is that the partial deregulation of access in competitive areas can be suboptimal. Duplication-based regulation creates more certainty both for firms and regulators and leads to greater welfare, provided that the regulator is fully informed and can fully commit to setting different prices. However, the regulator may suffer from information asymmetry and commitment problems. In this case, competition-based regulation may become the only feasible alternative to uniform prices. In conclusion, they show that compared to uniform access pricing, the adoption of geographically differentiated access prices can improve welfare and investment.

203. This chapter is also related to the literature on wholesale competition between vertically integrated firms. Ordover and Shafer (2007) consider a framework where one of the vertically integrated firms has a larger customer base than the other. The new entrant can enter the market only "service-based", and in two different ways. Either it can engage in "own-supplier cannibalisation" (i.e. cannibalise only the sales of its upstream supplier), or in "proportional cannibalisation" (i.e. cannibalise the sales of the two integrated firms in equal proportions). They find that there is entry in equilibrium and that the wholesale market is perfectly competitive in the latter case, whereas the entrant remains out of the market in the former case (as no integrated firm makes a wholesale offer). This is because, in the former case, the benefits from selling in the wholesale market (i.e. wholesale profits) do not compensate for the costs associated with it (i.e. the reduction of retail profits).

Brito and Pereira (2010) examine a different setting with circular differentiation between downstream firms , and obtain similar results. Bourreau, Hombert, Pouyet and Schutz (2011) consider a model of two-tier competition between two vertically integrated firms and one unintegrated downstream firm. They show there are equilibria where the wholesale market is not competitive.

204. This chapter is also related to the literature on mixed oligopolies. Merill and Schneider (1966) show that the existence of a public firm in an oligopolistic industry can result in improved market performance, with lower prices and increased output. Beato and Mas-Colell (1984) examine a mixed duopoly where the public firm takes as given the output of the private firm and is instructed by the government to use marginal cost pricing when choosing its own level of output. At the same time, the private firm acts as a leader maximising its profits along the public firm's reaction function. The main conclusion of their analysis is that such behaviour sometimes leads to higher social welfare than what could be obtained in the traditional second-best approach. De Fraja and Delbono (1989) investigate an industry formed by a single public firm and several private firms. They find that social welfare may be higher if the public firm is instructed to maximise profits rather than total surplus. Cremer, Marchand et Thisse (1989) examine to what extent a public firm is a relevant instrument to regulate an oligopolistic market. They find that the nationalisation of a single firm in an industry with only private firms can be socially optimal. However, if there are several existing public firms, higher total surplus is likely to be achieved if all but one of the public firms are privatised.

205. While the above cited papers consider public firms that maximise total welfare, other studies consider public firms that maximise a weighted sum of profits and consumer surplus. Matsumura (1998) considers partial privatisation with a duopoly involving a private firm and a privatised firm which is jointly owned by the public and private sectors. The author finds that full nationalisation (i.e. the government holds all shares in the firm) is not optimal unless the public firm is a monopolist. This suggests that in the context of a mixed oligopoly, the public firm should be (at least partially) privatised. On the other hand, he finds that full privatisation (i.e. the government sells all shares of the public firm) is not optimal if the public firm is as efficient as the private firm. This suggests that partial privatisation is a reasonable choice for the government in the context of a mixed oligopoly. Lee, Matsumura and Sato (2018) consider a framework where private firms first choose whether to enter the market and then the government chooses the degree of privatisation of the public firm. Their main finding is that the equilibrium degree of privatisation is too high (low) for both domestic and world welfare if private firms are domestic (foreign).

206. Another set of papers in the literature on mixed oligopolies considers public firms that maximise the sum of their profits and consumer surplus. Armstrong and Weeds (2007) study programme quality in digital television. They examine the case of a private duopoly and then consider a mixed duopoly where a private broadcaster competes with a public broadcaster. They show that the public firm obtains a larger audience and broadcasts less advertising than the private competitor. However, the public firm does not necessarily broadcast programmes of higher quality.

207. Jullien, Pouyet and Sand-Zantman (2010) analyze the relationship between a national regulator, an incumbent and a local firm investing in a new network.

They model a country divided into "districts", which differ by the level of demand for new services and the cost of building a new network. In a sequential game, the authors examine whether local government intervention in the network infrastructure should be limited so that private investments are not crowded out. Due to externalities, the investment decision of the local government in one district may influence the profitability of the private investment in another district. The authors takes into account that the incumbent operates under asymmetric information (since it cannot foresee the investment decision of the local government). They also consider that the objectives of the regulator and the local government may diverge since the regulator maximises not only the municipal agents' welfare. They find that public investment can be efficient in white areas, but that a ban on local government intervention can be welfare-enhancing in grey areas in presence of externalities, asymmetric information or conflicting goals between regulator and local governments. Therefore, the national regulator has to consider these issues when designing rules for investment of local governments.[82] In the same vein, Jullien, Pouyet and Sand-Zantman (2018) study the link between private firms' incentives to invest and public intervention.

208. In a recent empirical contribution, Wilson (2021) investigates to what extent public competition from local governments may crowd in or crowd out private investment in broadband infrastructures. He uses nationwide US data to estimate a dynamic oligopoly model. Wilson finds that public competition decreases the probability of private investment due to a crowding-out effect. However, it increases the probability of private investment through a preemption effect. The overall effect is that public investment crowds out more private investments than it induces through pre-emption. However, he finds that a ban on public investment in 30 U.S. states would result in total welfare loss of $18.78 billion over 20 years. Wilson (2017) concludes that banning public provision of internet access increases the profits of incumbent private firms at the expense of both consumers and local governments.

209. Finally, this chapter is related to the literature discussing public intervention and investment in new networks. Cave and Martin (2010) analyze the main motives of public investment and show that industrial policy, equity objectives and economic recovery are the main ones. They also question the means of public intervention by studying three broadband plans: Australia, New Zealand and Singapore. Hauge, Jamison and Gentry (2008) compare the types of markets that municipally owned telecommunications providers in the United States serve to the types of markets that competitive local exchange carriers (CLECs) serve. They find that CLECs focus on potential profitability, while municipalities appear to respond to other factors (e.g. political considerations). Thus, they find that municipal providers tend to serve markets that CLECs do not target, and therefore the presence of a municipal provider in a market does not affect the probability that a CLEC also serves that market. Their results suggest that municipalities may not pose a significant competitive threat to CLECs and do not preclude CLEC participation. Briglauer,

82 In a more general treatment, Jullien, Pouyet and Sand-Zantman (2017) examine the possibility that the local government reaches different types of contractual agreements with the incumbent.

Holzleitner and Vogelsang (2016) question the contract practice of determining ex ante targets of network expansion by governments. Due to information asymmetry and uncertainty, they show that delegating the choice of network expansion to a better-informed network operator is efficient.

3. Model

210. We consider a country composed of different areas $z \in [0,\infty)$, with identical demand but different sunk costs of being covered with a network infrastructure. The cost of covering an area $z \in [0,\infty)$ is $c(z)$, with $c'(z) > 0$, $c(0) = 0$, and $\lim_{z\to\infty} c(z) = +\infty$. The total cost of covering the areas from 0 to z is then $C(z) = \int_0^z c(x)dx$, with $C'(z) = c(z) \geq 0$ and $C''(z) = c'(z) > 0$.

211. A private firm competes with public firms in coverage and prices all over the country. The private firm, firm P, makes its decisions in order to maximise its profit, whereas public firms maximise the sum of their profit and consumer surplus under a budget constraint.[83] We consider two types of public firms: (i) a national public firm, firm N, which decides on prices and coverage for the whole country; and (ii) local public firms based in each area z, making independent price and coverage decisions, which we all call L for simplicity. We assume that all firms, be they private or public, have the same constant marginal cost of production, which we normalise to zero.

212. Depending on the coverage decisions of the firms, each local market can have no provider, a monopoly provider, or two competing providers. The monopoly demand in a local market for a given price p, $D^m(p)$, is the same for all firms $i \in \{P,N,L\}$, and we denote by $D_i^d(p_i, p_j)$ the duopoly demand for firm i, where p_i denotes the price of firm i and p_j the price of the rival firm j. Firms offer differentiated products. The monopoly demand is downward-sloping, and as usual we assume that a firm's demand decreases in its own price ($\partial D_i^d(p_i, p_j)/\partial p_i \leq 0$) and increases in its rival's price ($\partial D_i^d(p_i, p_j)/\partial p_j \geq 0$). Finally, the duopoly demands are symmetric: $D_i^d(p_i, p_j) = D_j^d(p_i, p_j)$.

213. We assume that the private firm P and the national public firm N set a uniform price that applies to all their covered areas in the country, which is a standard business practice in network industries. By contrast, each local public firm L sets a price that applies only locally, and depends on the market conditions in the area.

214. We assume away any subsidies for public deployment of infrastructures; the difference in coverage and pricing incentives between the private firm and the public firms thus only stems from the difference of objective functions.

---

83 The public firm cares about its own profit and consumer surplus, but not about the private firm's profit. This assumption about the public firm's objective function is in line with, e.g. Matsumura (1998), Armstrong and Weeds (2007) and Jullien, Pouyet and Sand-Zantman (2010).

215. Social welfare in a given area, gross of investment costs, is defined as the sum of firms' profits and consumer surplus, and denoted by $w^m(p_i)$ and $w^d(p_i,p_j)$ for a monopoly area and a duopoly area, respectively. We assume that it is decreasing in prices, that is, $\partial w^m(p_i)/\partial p_i \leq 0$ and $\partial w^d(p_i,p_j)/\partial p_k \leq 0$, for $k = i, j$.

216. Finally, we make the following assumption on profits:

217. **Assumption 1.** *The monopoly profit $pD^m(p)$ and the duopoly profit $p_iD_i^d(p_i,p_j)$ are concave in prices.*

218. We denote the optimal monopoly price by $p^m = \text{argmax}_p pD^m(p)$ and the monopoly profit by $\pi^m \equiv p^m D^m(p^m)$. Moreover, let $BR^d(p_j) \equiv \text{argmax}_p pD_i^d(p,p_j)$ denote the duopoly best-response, for $j \neq i$. We assume that prices are strategic complements. The equilibrium in duopoly is assumed to exist and be unique; the duopoly price is given by $p^d = BR^d(BR^d(p_i))$ and the duopoly profit is $\pi^d \equiv p^d D(p^d,p^d)$.

219. We study the coverage-price game where firms decide simultaneously on coverage and prices. We look for the Nash equilibrium of this game.

4. Monopoly benchmark

220. In this section, we solve for the equilibrium of the coverage-price game in a monopoly benchmark, where only one firm, private or public, is active. We study the equilibrium outcome under monopoly with (i) a private firm, (ii) a national public firm, and (iii) local public firms.

221. **Private firm.** The private firm, P, decides on a uniform price, p, and a coverage, z, to maximise its profit, which is given by:[84]

$$\Pi_P = zpD^m(p) - C(z). \tag{1}$$

222. Firm P covers the areas from 0 to z for a total investment cost $C(z)$, and obtains the monopoly profit $pD^m(p)$ in each covered area. Its optimal coverage and price decisions are then as follows.

223. **Lemma 1.** *The monopoly private firm sets the monopoly price $P_P^m = p^m$ and covers up to the area $Z_P^m = z^m$, with $z^m = c^{-1}(\pi^m)$.*

224. *Proof.* For a given coverage z, firm P's profit, which is given by (1), is maximised at the monopoly price $p = p^m$. Replacing for $p = p^m$ into (1), the optimal coverage for the private firm is then given by $c(z) = p^m D^m(p^m) = \pi^m$, i.e. $z = c^{-1}(\pi^m) \equiv z^m$.

---

84 Note that in this monopoly benchmark, the private firm has no incentive to price discriminate between areas since the demand is the same in all areas.

225. The private firm sets the monopoly price in all covered areas, since it maximises its local profits. It then covers up to a marginal area when the marginal private benefit from investment (the monopoly profit) is equal to the marginal cost of investment.

226. **National public firm.** The national public firm, N, chooses a uniform price, p, and a coverage, z, to maximise the sum of its profit and consumer surplus, less the investment cost:

$$W_N = zw^m(p) - C(z), \tag{2}$$

subject to the budget constraint $zpD^m(p) - C(z) \geq 0$. Note that in this monopoly framework, the sum of N's profit and consumer surplus corresponds to social welfare.

227. **Lemma 2.** *Under monopoly, the national public firm sets the uniform price* $P_N^m \leq p^m$ *and covers up to the area* $Z_N^m > z^m$, *with* $w^m\left(P_N^m\right) = c\left(Z_N^m\right)$ *and* $Z_N^m P_N^m D^m\left(P_N^m\right) - C\left(Z_N^m\right) = 0$.

228. *Proof.* Consider first firm N's pricing decision for a given coverage z. From our assumptions, for a given coverage z, total welfare, which is given by (2), is decreasing in the price p, whereas the public firm's profit, $zpD^m(p) - C(z)$, is increasing in p, up to the monopoly price p^m. Firm N thus sets the minimum price such that its budget constraint still holds. Let $\underline{p}_N(z)$ denote the lowest price p such that $zpD^m(p) - C(z) \geq 0$. The limit price $\underline{p}_N(z)$ exists if and only if $z\pi^m \geq C(z)$. If this price exists, N's optimal price, for a given coverage z, is $p_N = \underline{p}_N(z)$. If $\underline{p}_N(z)$ does not exist, there is no price allowing the firm to break even while covering the areas from 0 to z.

229. Using the implicit function theorem on the budget constraint and the fact that $c' > 0$, we find that $\partial \underline{p}_N(z) / \partial z \geq 0$. Furthermore, we have $\underline{p}_N(z) \leq p^m$. Intuitively, if the public firm covers a larger part of the country, it must set a higher uniform price to break even. This price cannot be larger than p^m, since the monopoly profit is decreasing for $p \geq p^m$.

230. Consider now firm N's choice of coverage for a given uniform price p. Using (2), N's optimal coverage is the solution of $w^m(p) = c(z)$. The optimal coverage for the public firm is then the solution of $w^m\left(\underline{p}_N(z)\right) = c(z)$. Since $\underline{p}_N(z)$ is increasing in z and $w(p)$ is decreasing in p, $w^m\left(\underline{p}_N(z)\right)$ is decreasing in z, whereas $c(z)$ is increasing in z, with $c(0) = 0$ and $\lim_{z \to \infty} c(z) = +\infty$. Therefore, there exists a unique Z_N^m such that $w^m\left(\underline{p}_N\left(Z_N^m\right)\right) = c\left(Z_N^m\right)$. The public firm's optimal uniform price is then $P_N^m = \underline{p}_N\left(Z_N^m\right)$.

231. Finally, we have $P_N^m \leq p^m$ as $P_N^m = \underline{p}_N\left(Z_N^m\right)$ and $\underline{p}_N(z) \leq p^m$ for all z. Furthermore, since $w^m(p)$ is decreasing and $\underline{p}_N\left(Z_N^m\right) \leq p^m$, Z_N^m is larger than the coverage z' defined by $w^m\left(p^m\right) = c(z')$. Since $w^m\left(p^m\right) > p^m D^m\left(p^m\right) = c\left(z^m\right)$, $z' > z^m$ and hence $Z_N^m > z^m$.

232. The public firm covers the areas where the marginal social benefit of investment is greater than the marginal cost of investment, taking into account the uniform price that allows it to break even. This price depends on the marginal area covered, and increases with the level of coverage. As a consequence, the marginal social benefit of investment decreases as the public firm covers more outlying areas. Equilibrium coverage is then defined by the intersection of the (decreasing) marginal social return to investment with the (increasing) marginal investment cost.

233. **Local public firms.** Finally, we investigate the case where a continuum of local public firms, based in all the areas of the country, decide independently on the coverage of their area and the local price of the service. We define as $\Im(z) \in \{0,1\}$ the investment strategy of firm *L*, based in area *z*, where $\Im(z) = 1$ if *L* invests, and $\Im(z) = 0$ if it does not.

234. Let p_L denote firm *L*'s price in local area *z*, conditional on coverage. Firm *L*'s objective is to maximise the local area's welfare, which is given by

$$\Im(z)\left[w^m(p_L) - c(z)\right], \tag{3}$$

subject to the local budget constraint

$$p_L D^m(p_L) - c(z) \geq 0. \tag{4}$$

235. **Lemma 3.** *Under monopoly, local public firms set the price* $P_L^m(z)$*, which is increasing in* *z, so that their local budget constraint binds, and cover up to the area* $Z_L^m = z^m$.

236. *Proof.* Consider first firm *L*'s pricing decision in a given area *z*. Since $\partial w^m(p) / \partial p < 0$, firm *L* sets the lowest price compatible with its budget constraint (4). Let $\underline{p}_L(z)$ denote the lowest price such that $p_L D^m(p_L) - c(z) \geq 0$, which exists if and only if $\pi^m \geq c(z)$. If it exists, firm *L*'s optimal price for a given coverage *z* is $p_L = \underline{p}_L(z)$. Since the investment cost *c*(*z*) is increasing, $\underline{p}_L(z)$ is increasing too.

237. Note that $\underline{p}_L(z) > \underline{p}_N(z)$. Indeed, the budget constraint for *N* can be written as $p_N D^m(p_N) - C(z) / z \geq 0$, and

$$c(z) - \frac{C(z)}{z} = \frac{1}{z}\int_0^z (c(z) - c(t))dt > 0,$$

as $c' > 0$. We now solve for firm *L*'s coverage decision. Replacing for $\underline{p}_L(z)$ into (3) and (4), firm *L* decides to invest if and only if

$$w^m\left(\underline{p}_L(z)\right) - c(z) \geq 0, \quad \text{with} \quad \underline{p}_L(z) D^m\left(\underline{p}_L(z)\right) - c(z) = 0, \tag{5}$$

that is, the local public firm invests if the social benefit from investment is larger than the investment cost, for a price set so that it just breaks even.

238. We find that *L* invests if and only if $z \leq z^m$. Indeed, the maximum gross profit that *L* can make is the monopoly profit π^m, and therefore, the marginal area such that the budget constraint is satisfied is the monopoly area z^m. In this area, we have $w^m\left(p^m\right) - c\left(z^m\right) > 0$, since $w^m\left(p^m\right) = \pi^m + CS\left(p^m\right) > \pi^m = c\left(z_m\right)$.

Hence, L invests if and only if $z \leq z^m = Z_L^m$. If it does, it sets the local price $P_L^m(z) = \underline{p}_L(z)$ defined above.

239. A local public firm L invests only if it can break even. Since the maximum profit it can earn is the monopoly profit, the marginal area with local public firms is the monopoly area z^m. In covered areas, each local public firm sets a price that allows it to break even. The price of the service becomes higher as we move towards more remote areas, because local public firms have to charge a higher price to cover the higher investment cost.

240. **Comparison.** We can now compare the market outcome in the three scenarios, with a private firm, a national public firm and local public firms, in terms of total coverage and prices. Using Lemmas 1-3 above, we obtain the following result.

241. **Proposition 1** *In the monopoly benchmark, the market outcome is as follows:*

(i) Total coverage is larger with a national public firm, but it is the same with a private firm or local public firms (i.e. $Z_N^m > Z_P^m = Z_L^m = z^m$).

(ii) The national public firm sets a lower uniform price than the private firm, while the local public firms set local prices that depend on the area and can be either lower or higher than the price set by the national public firm (i.e. $P_N^m < P_P^m = p^m$, while $P_L^m(z) \leq P_N^m$ if z is sufficiently low, and $P_L^m(z) > P_N^m$ otherwise).

242. The private firm deploys its infrastructure in all the areas $z \leq z^m$ where the monopoly profit covers the investment cost. Due to their local budget constraints, the investment incentives of local public firms are similar. Since a local public firm invests only if it can break even, the marginal area for local public firms is the area where the largest profit, that is, the monopoly profit, is obtained, that is, area z^m. By contrast, the national public firm covers a larger share of the territory. This is because it has a global budget constraint, and can therefore cross-subsidise investment in high-cost areas with profits obtained in low-cost areas.

243. We can also compare the market outcome in the three different scenarios in terms of total welfare. Since total coverage is larger with a national public firm than with a private firm ($Z_N^m > Z_P^m$) and prices are lower ($P_N^m < P_P^m$), total welfare is larger with a national public firm than with a private firm ($W_N^m > W_P^m$). Similarly, total coverage is the same with a private firm or with local public firms, but prices are (at least weakly) lower in the latter case, so total welfare is larger with local public firms than with a private firm ($W_L^m > W_P^m$). The comparison of total welfare with a national public firm and local public firms is ambiguous. On the one hand, total coverage is wider with a national public firm. On the other, prices are lower with local public firms in low-cost areas, but higher in high-cost areas.

244. To illustrate Proposition 1, we adopt a specific Shubik-Levitan demand model and set $c(z) = z$ to compute the equilibrium coverage and prices (see Appendix A for details). Figure 2 shows, for the three scenarios, prices on the left and total coverage on the right. Since $c(0) = 0$, the price set by the local public firm at

$z = 0$ is equal to marginal cost, that is, zero with our normalisation. The price of local public firms then increases as we move towards costlier areas, until it reaches the monopoly price p^m.

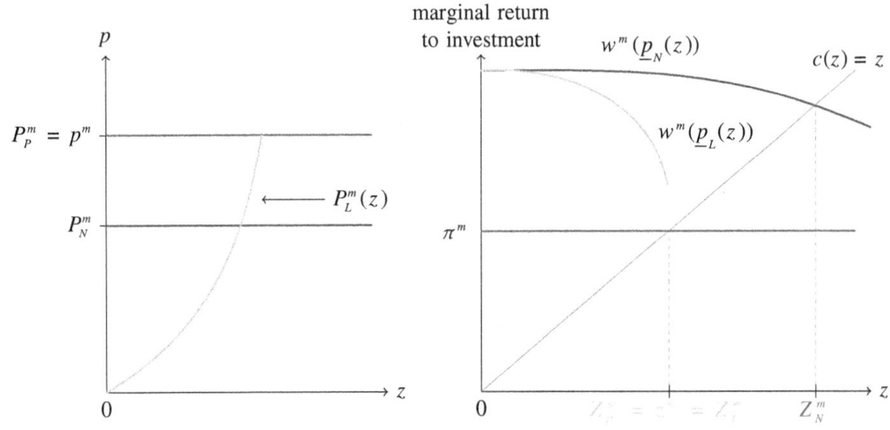

Figure 2 – Level of prices (left) and total coverage (right) in the monopoly benchmark

245. On the right-hand side, the equilibrium coverage of the private firm, $Z_P^m = z^m$, is given by the intersection of the marginal private return to investment, π^m, with the marginal investment cost, $c(z)$. Similarly, the equilibrium coverage of the national public firm, Z_N^m, is given by the intersection of the marginal social return to investment, $w^m\left(P_N^m(z)\right)$, with the marginal investment cost, $c(z)$. The marginal social return to investment is decreasing in z, because the public firm has to increase its uniform price when it covers a larger territory. Finally, notice that the marginal social return to investment for local public firms does not intersect with the marginal investment cost; this is because total coverage with local public firms is determined by the budget constraint of the marginal area.

246. In this specific Shubik-Levitan linear model, we find that $W_N^m > W_L^m > W_P^m$, that is, total welfare is the highest with a national public firm. In other words, it is better to set up a national entity to roll out a new infrastructure than to delegate this task to independent local authorities.

247. Note that this benchmark model can be readily extended to incorporate subsidies. A subsidy S granted to a public firm relaxes its budget constraint. Since public firms set the lowest price compatible with their budget constraint, subsidies thus lead to lower prices. This, in turn, increases the marginal social return to investment, and therefore public firms also expand their coverage when they receive subsidies.

5. Private Firm vs National Public Firm

248. In this section, we analyze the competition in coverage and prices between a private firm and a national public firm.

249. In this coverage-price game, two equilibria can emerge *a priori*: one where the national public firm leads in investment (that is, invests more than its rival), and another one where the private firm leads in investment. In the context of this chapter, it makes sense to consider that the private firm concentrates on low-cost areas, whereas the public firm covers a larger territory, expanding coverage to outlying and costlier areas. We thus focus the analysis on the case where the public firm leads in investment, that is, where $z_N > z_P$ in equilibrium. We solve for the equilibrium of the coverage-price game under this assumption.[85]

5.1. Pricing strategies

250. We start by determining the equilibrium prices of firms P and N for given coverage levels z_N and z_P, with $z_N > z_P$.

251. **Best responses.** Consider first the pricing decision of the private firm. Firm P chooses a price p_P to maximise its profit, which is given by

$$\Pi_P = z_P p_P D_P^d(p_P, p_N) - C(z_P). \tag{6}$$

252. Firm P incurs the total investment cost $C(z_P)$ to cover the areas from 0 to z_P. In each of these areas, it competes with firm N, and obtains the duopoly profit $p_P D_P^d(p_P, p_N)$. From (6), firm P's best-response to a price p_N is the duopoly best-response, $p_P = BR^d(p_N)$.

253. Consider now the decision of the public firm. Firm N chooses its price p_N to maximise its objective function, which is given by

$$\Pi_N = (z_N - z_P)w^m(p_N) + z_P\left(p_N D_N^d(p_N, p_P) + CS(p_N, p_P)\right) - C(z_N), \tag{7}$$

subject to the budget constraint

$$(z_N - z_P)p_N D^m(p_N) + z_P p_N D_N^d(p_N, p_P) \geq C(z_N). \tag{8}$$

254. Since it leads in investment, firm N is a (public) monopoly in the areas z_P to z_N, where it cares about total local welfare. In the areas 0 to z_P, firm N competes with firm P; in these areas, it cares about the sum of its duopoly profit and consumer surplus.

255. **Lemma 4.** *The best-response of the national public firm N is to set the lowest price such that its budget constraint* (8) *is binding, that is,* $p_N^{BR}(p_P) = \underline{p}_N^d(p_P, z_P, z_N)$, *where* $\underline{p}_N^d$ *satisfies* $(z_N - z_P)\underline{p}_N^d D^m\left(\underline{p}_N^d\right) + z_P \underline{p}_N^d D_N^d\left(\underline{p}_N^d, p_P\right) = C(z_N)$.

---

[85] The case where the private firm leads in investment is discussed in Appendix B.1.

256. *Proof.* We first show that the objective function of the public firm, which is given by (7), is decreasing in p_N. This is because, (i) $w^m(p_N)$ is decreasing in p_N from our assumptions, and (ii) $p_N D_N^d(p_N, p_P) + CS(p_N, p_P)$ is decreasing in p_N too. To prove point (ii), we rewrite $p_N D_N^d(p_N, p_P) + CS(p_N, p_P) = w^d(p_N, p_P) - p_P D_P^d(p_P, p_N)$. Therefore,

$$\frac{\partial\left[p_N D_N^d(p_N, p_P) + CS(p_N, p_P)\right]}{\partial p_N} = \underbrace{\frac{\partial w^d(p_N, p_P)}{\partial p_N}}_{\leq 0} - p_P \underbrace{\frac{\partial D_P^d(p_P, p_N)}{\partial p_N}}_{\geq 0} \leq 0.$$

257. The public firm thus sets the lowest price compatible with its budget constraint. From Assumption 1, pD^m (p) and $p_N D_N^d(p_N, p_P)$ are concave, which implies that the budget constraint (8) is concave in p_N too.
Let $\hat{p}_i(p_j) \equiv \text{argmax}_p z_j p D_i^d(p, p_j) + (z_i - z_j) p D^m(p)$. We have $\hat{p}_N(p_P) \in \left[BR^d(p_P), p^m\right]$. The left-hand side of the budget constraint (8) is then increasing in p_N for $p_N \in [0, \hat{p}_N]$. For given coverage z_N and z_P, we define $\underline{p}_N^d(p_P, z_P, z_N)$ such that $z_P \underline{p}_N^d D_N^d(\underline{p}_N^d, p_P) + (z_N - z_P)\underline{p}_N^d D^m(\underline{p}_N^d) = C(z_N)$. This price $\underline{p}_N^d$ exists if and only if firm *N* breaks even when it sets its profit-maximising price, that is, if $z_P \hat{p}_N D_N^d(\hat{p}_N, p_P) + (z_N - z_P)\hat{p}_N D^m(\hat{p}_N) \geq C(z_N)$. Firm *N*'s best-response to a price p_P set by the private firm is then $p_N^{BR}(p_P) = \underline{p}_N^d(p_P, z_P, z_N)$, with $\underline{p}_N^d \leq \hat{p}_N$.

258. The public firm best responds to a price p_P set by the private firm by setting the lowest price compatible with its budget constraint, and this price is lower than or equal to the uniform price that maximises its total profit (i.e. $\hat{p}_N$). Note that if at the profit-maximising price $\hat{p}_N$, firm *N* does not break even, there is no best-response to the price set by the private firm.

259. The following lemma shows how the firms react to a price increase of their rival:

260. **Lemma 5.** *Whereas firm P reacts to a price increase of its rival by increasing its own price (strategic complementarity), firm N reacts to a price increase of its rival by decreasing its own price (strategic substituability).*

261. *Proof.* The first point of the proposition simply re-states our assumption that prices are strategic complements in a duopoly with two private firms. To prove the second point, let $BC(p_N, p_P) \equiv z_P p_N D_N^d(p_N, p_P) + (z_N - z_P) p_N D^m(p_N) - C(z_N)$ represent the budget constraint of the public firm. Firm *N*'s best-response satisfies $BC\left(p_N^{BR}, p_P\right) = 0$. From the implicit function theorem, we have

$$\frac{\partial p_N^{BR}}{\partial p_P} = -\left.\frac{\partial BC / \partial p_P}{\partial BC / \partial p_N}\right|_{p_N = p_N^{BR}}.$$

262. Since $p_N^{BR} \le \hat{p}_N$, we have $\partial BC / \partial p_N|_{p_N = p_N^{BR}} \ge 0$. Furthermore, we have

$$\left.\frac{\partial BC}{\partial p_P}\right|_{p_N = p_N^{BR}} = z_P p_N^{BR} \frac{\partial D_N}{\partial p_P} \ge 0.$$

263. This proves that $\partial p_N^{BR} / \partial p_P \le 0$.

264. The intuition of this result is that when the private firm increases its price, its demand decreases while the demand, and hence the profit, of the public firm increases. Since the public firm sets the minimum price satisfying its budget constraint, it reacts by decreasing its price. This result shows that compared to the monopoly benchmark with a national public firm, entry and competition from a private firm leads the public firm to *increase* its price.

265. **Equilibrium prices.** For given coverage levels, the equilibrium prices P_P and P_N are given by the intersection of the best responses of the private firm and the public firm. If the intersection exists, it is unique, since best responses are continuous, the best response of the private firm is increasing and the best response of the public firm is decreasing. For the rest of the discussion, we assume that this intersection exists.[86] Below, we will discuss this assumption for the linear Shubik-Levitan demand model.

266. To study how coverage affects pricing decisions, we define $\sigma \equiv z_P / z_N \in (0,1)$ as the ratio of coverage levels. The ratio σ can be interpreted as the overlap between the private firm's and the public firm's covered territories. If σ is low, it means that P covers a small territory compared to N, and we are close to the scenario of a national public monopoly. Conversely, if σ is close to 1, this means that P covers (almost) as much territory as N, and we are close to the scenario of a mixed duopoly all over the country. The equilibrium prices can then be written as functions of z_N and σ: $P_P = P_P(z_N, \sigma)$ and $P_N = P_N(z_N, \sigma)$.

267. The following proposition characterises how the coverage by firm N and the degree of overlap between firm P's and firm N's networks affect equilibrium prices.

268. **Proposition 2.** *Assume that the price equilibrium exists, for given coverage levels.*

- *For a given coverage z_N by the national public firm, firms' equilibrium prices P_P and P_N increase with the ratio of coverage levels $\sigma = z_P / z_N$ (i.e. with z_P).*
- *For a given coverage z_P by the private firm, equilibrium prices increase when the public firm covers a larger territory (z_N increases) if and only if $P_N D^m(P_N) \ge c(z_N)$.*

---

86 We can provide a necessary and sufficient condition for the best responses to intersect. Let $\widehat{BC} = BC(\hat{p}_N(p_P))$, where BC is the budget constraint (i.e. profit) of the public firm. We have $\partial \widehat{BC} / \partial p_P \ge 0$. If this derivative is positive at $p_P = 0$, it is positive for all $p_P \ge 0$, and the intersection of best responses always exists. If $\partial \widehat{BC} / \partial p_P |_{p_P = 0} < 0$, there exists $\underline{p}_P$ such that $\widehat{BC}(\underline{p}_P) = 0$. The intersection of best responses exists in this case if and only if $BR^d(\hat{p}_N(\underline{p}_P)) \ge \underline{p}_P$.

269. *Proof.* For given coverage levels, and hence, for a given ratio $\sigma = z_P / z_N$, firms' equilibrium prices are the solution of the following system of equations:

$$A \equiv (z_N - z_P) p_N D^m(p_N) + z_P p_N D_N^d(p_N, p_P) - C(z_N) = 0,$$

$$B \equiv D_P^d(p_P, p_N) + p_P \frac{\partial D_P^d(p_P, p_N)}{\partial p_P} = 0.$$

270. The first equation, which defines firm *N*'s best response, corresponds to the budget constraint of the public firm, whereas the second equation is the first-order condition for firm *P*. Using Cramer's rule, we find that

$$\frac{\partial P_N}{\partial z_P} = \frac{-p^N\left(D^m(P_N) - D_N^d(P_N, P_P)\right)}{D} \frac{\partial^2 \pi_P^d}{\partial p_P^2},$$

$$\frac{\partial P_P}{\partial z_P} = \frac{p^N\left(D^m(P_N) - D_N^d(P_N, P_P)\right)}{D} \frac{\partial^2 \pi_P^d}{\partial p_P p_N},$$

where

$$D = \underbrace{\frac{\partial A}{\partial p_P}}_{(+)} \underbrace{\frac{\partial B}{\partial p_N}}_{(+)} - \underbrace{\frac{\partial A}{\partial p_N}}_{(+)} \underbrace{\frac{\partial B}{\partial p_P}}_{(-)} > 0.$$

271. Since at the equilibrium prices, $\partial^2 \pi_P^d / \partial p_P^2 \leq 0$ (concavity), $\partial^2 \pi_P^d / \partial p_P p_N \geq 0$ (strategic complementarity), and $D^m(P_N) > D_N^d(P_N, P_P)$, we have $\partial P_N / \partial z_P \geq 0$ and $\partial P_P / \partial z_P \geq 0$, and hence for a given z_N, $\partial P_N / \partial \sigma \geq 0$ and $\partial P_P / \partial \sigma \geq 0$.

272. Using a similar approach, we find that $\partial P_N / \partial z_N \geq 0$ and $\partial P_P / \partial z_N \geq 0$ if $P_N D^m(P_N) \leq c(z_N)$; otherwise, if $P_N D^m(P_N) \geq c(z_N)$, then $\partial P_N / \partial z_N \leq 0$ and $\partial P_P / \partial z_N \leq 0$.

273. Proposition 2 states the counterintuitive result that more intense competition through a larger overlap between the private and public firms' networks drives firms' prices *up*. When the overlap increases, the best response of the private firm, which corresponds to the duopoly best response, is unchanged. By contrast, the best response of the public firm shifts outwards. The idea is that when the duopoly areas expand to the detriment of the monopoly areas, the ability of the public firm to cross-subsidise between low-cost and high-cost areas is lessened. Firm *N* has to increase its uniform price, and due to strategic complementarity, firm *P* does the same, which leads to higher equilibrium prices.

274. The second point of the proposition shows that when the public firm extends its coverage, how prices adjust depends on the profitability of the marginal (monopoly) area. If the marginal area is profitable, the public firm can use the incremental profit to reduce its uniform price. Conversely, if it is unprofitable, the public firm has to increase its uniform price to break even. In both cases,

the private firm follows the price reaction of the public firm, due to strategic complementarity.

5.2. Coverage strategies

275. We now consider the coverage decisions of firms N and P, for given prices p_N and p_P. From (6) and (7), the equilibrium coverage levels are solutions to the system of first-order conditions,[87]

$$p_P D_P^d(p_P, p_N) = c(z_P),$$
$$w^m(p_N) = c(z_N).$$

276. Replacing for $p_N = P_N(z_P, z_N)$ and $p_P = P_P(z_P, z_N)$, the equilibrium coverage of firms N and P are the solution of

$$P_P(z_P, z_N) D_P^d(P_P(z_P, z_N), P_N(z_P, z_N)) = c(z_P), \tag{9}$$

$$w^m(P_N(z_P, z_N)) = c(z_N). \tag{10}$$

277. We assume that the equilibrium exists and is unique, and denote by Z_P^n and Z_N^n the equilibrium coverage of the private firm and the public firm, respectively. The following proposition compares the equilibrium outcome with the monopoly benchmark.

278. **Proposition 3.** *Assume that the equilibrium to the coverage-price game exists and is unique. In equilibrium,*

   (i) the private firm P covers a smaller territory than in the benchmark and charges a lower price, i.e. $Z_P^n < Z_P^m$ *and* $P_P^n < P_P^m$*;*

   (ii) the public firm N covers a smaller territory than in the benchmark and charges either a lower or a higher price, i.e. $Z_N^n < Z_N^m$ *and* $P_N^n \gtreqless P_N^m$.

279. *Proof.* First, we compare the equilibrium coverage levels to the benchmark. The private firm's coverage is given by the first-order condition, $P_P^n D_P^d(P_P^n, P_N^n) = c(Z_P^n)$. Since $P_P^n D_P^d(P_P^n, P_N^n) < \pi^m$, then $Z_P^n < c^{-1}(\pi^m) = Z_P^m$. Using (10), we see that since P_N increases with z_P (from Proposition 4) and $w^m(\cdot)$ is decreasing, a higher z_P leads to a lower coverage z_N by the public firm. Since for $z_P = 0$, the public firm sets the benchmark coverage z^N, this proves that $Z_N^n < Z_N^m$.

280. Second, we compare the equilibrium prices to the prices in the benchmark. Firm N's equilibrium price satisfies $P_N^n = \underline{p}_N^d(P_P^n) \leq \hat{p}_N(P_P^n) < p^m$. Since $P_N^n < p^m$, we have $P_P^n = BR^d(P_N^n) < p^m = P_P^m$. As for the public firm, in the benchmark, firm N's price is given by

$$Z_N^m P_N^m D^m(P_N^m) = C(Z_N^m).$$

---

[87] The second-order conditions are satisfied as $c' > 0$.

281. In the duopoly setting, firm N's equilibrium price satisfies $P_N^n = \underline{p}_N^d\left(P_P^n\right)$, that is,

$$Z_N^n P_N^n D^m\left(P_N^n\right) - \underbrace{Z_P^n\left(P_N^n D^m\left(P_N^n\right) - P_N^n D_N^d\left(P_N^n, P_P^n\right)\right)}_{\text{business-stealingeffect}} = C\left(Z_N^n\right).$$

282. Assume that $Z_N^n = Z_N^m$. Then, firm N has to set a higher price to break even in duopoly, which means that $P_N^n > P_N^m$. However, this effect is counter-balanced by the fact that N covers less in duopoly than in the monopoly benchmark (i.e. $Z_N^n < Z_N^m$). Its investment cost is thus lower, allowing a lower price to be set. Firm N's price can thus be either lower or higher in duopoly compared to the benchmark.

283. The proposition shows that the competition between the private firm and the public decreases coverage, compared to the monopoly benchmark. In particular, the public firm, which leads in investment, covers a smaller territory than in the benchmark. This is because, the competition from the private firm forces the public firm to set a higher price to break even. This decreases the marginal social benefit from investment, and thus the public firm covers less of the country than in the benchmark.

284. In terms of prices, the private firm sets a lower price than in the monopoly benchmark, due to the competition from the public firm. The impact of the competition from the private firm on the public firm's price is ambiguous. On the one hand, there is a business stealing effect, which forces the public firm to increase its price. On the other, the competition leads the public firm to cover a smaller territory. Its investment cost is thus lower, allowing the public firm to set a lower price to break even.

5.3. Linear demand example

285. In the linear Shubik-Levitan demand model, for given coverage levels, firm P's best-response is the duopoly best-response,

$$p_P = BR^d\left(p_N\right) = \frac{2 + \gamma p_N}{2(2+\gamma)}, \tag{11}$$

286. whereas firm N's best-response is given by $p_N = \underline{p}_N^d\left(p_P, z_P, z_N\right)$, where $\underline{p}_N^d$ is the lowest price such that the budget constraint holds:

$$\underline{p}_N^d\left(p_P, z_P, z_N\right) = \hat{p}_N\left(p_P\right)\left(1 - \sqrt{1 - \frac{8C\left(z_N\right)}{\left(4z_N + z_P(\gamma p_P - 2)\right)\hat{p}_N\left(p_P\right)}}\right), \tag{12}$$

and $\hat{p}_N$ is the price that maximises N's profit,

$$\hat{p}_N\left(p_P\right) = \frac{4 + \sigma(\gamma p_P - 2)}{8 + 2\sigma(\gamma - 2)}.$$

287. Firm N's best-response to a given price p_P, $\underline{p}_N^d(\cdot)$, is defined if at the profit-maximising price $\hat{p}_N$, firm N breaks even.

288. The equilibrium prices P_P and P_N are then given by the intersection of the best-responses, given in (11) and (12).[88]

289. Figure 3 below shows the equilibrium prices for given coverage levels, for $\gamma = 1$, $C(z) = c_0 z^2 / 2$, $z_N = 10$, $\sigma \in [0,1]$, and $c_0 = 0.01$ (left) and $c_0 = 0.02$ (right). The figure on the left shows a case where equilibrium prices are always defined. On the figure on the right, by contrast, the equilibrium prices exist only if the degree of overlap is not too high. If the coverage of the private firm is close to that of the public firm, the public firm cannot break even when it sets its profit-maximising price. In this case, the competition between the private firm and the public firm is not sustainable. In both cases, prices increase with the degree of overlap σ, and the price charged by the private firm is also always higher than the price set by the public firm.

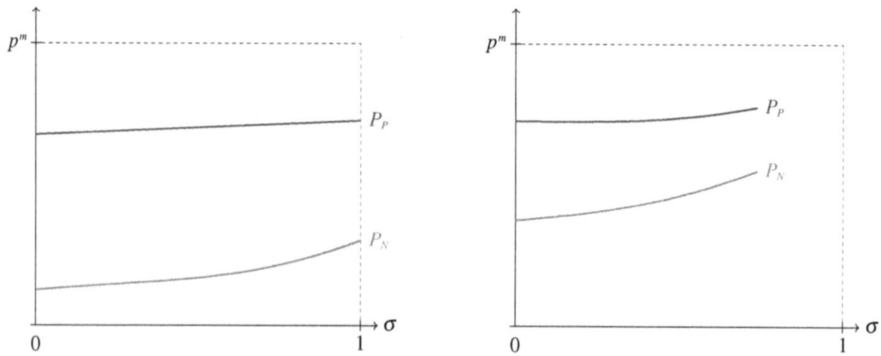

Figure 3 – Prices as a function of the ratio of coverage levels σ

290. Using (10), we compute the best response coverage for firm N to a coverage z_P by the private firm. Plugging this best response into the first-order condition (9), we solve for the equilibrium coverage levels Z_P^n and Z_N^n, which then gives the equilibrium prices.

291. Figure 4 shows the equilibrium prices and coverage levels as a function of the degree of substituability γ for the investment cost function $c(z) = c_0 z$, with $c_0 = 0.01$. We see that compared to the monopoly benchmark, competition between a private firm and a national public firm leads to lower coverage. However, competition tends to drive prices down. Note if the price charged by the public firm is lower with competition than in the monopoly benchmark, it is because in the former case the firm covers a smaller territory, and has thus lower costs to recover.

88 We omit the expressions of P_P and P_N, which are algebraically complex.

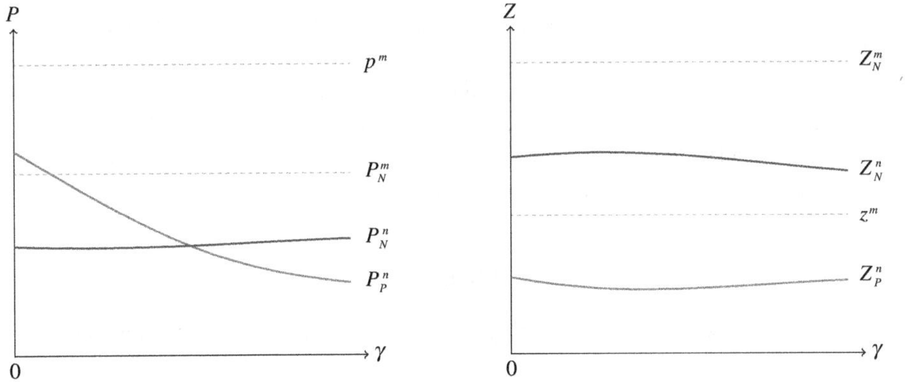

Figure 4 – Equilibrium price and coverage levels if the national public firm leads in investment

292. Figure 5 shows the equilibrium welfare as a function of the degree of substituability γ for the investment cost function $c(z) = c_0 z$, with $c_0 = 0.01$. We see that compared to the private monopoly, competition between a private and a national public firm leads to a lower welfare when competition is soft (i.e. low γ). Converserly, as competition intensifies, welfare is higher with a mixed duopoly. Note that while welfare under mixed duopoly is always lower than under national monopoly, we see that there is a level of γ for which welfare levels W_N^m and W^n are very close.

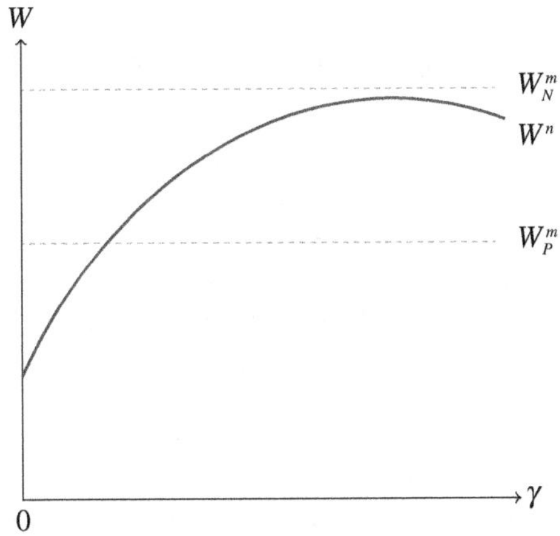

Figure 5 – Equilibrium welfare levels if the national public firm leads in investment

6. Private Firm vs Local Public Firms

293. This section studies the competition in prices and coverage between a private firm and local public firms. As in Section 5, we focus on the case where the local public firms lead in investment, that is, where $z_L \geq z_P$. We solve for the equilibrium of the coverage-price game under this assumption.[89]

6.1. Pricing strategies

294. To begin with, we analyze firms' pricing strategies for given coverage levels z_P and z_L, with $z_P \leq z_L$.

295. **Best responses.** Consider first the pricing decision of a local public firm L based in a given area $z \leq z_L$. We have to distinguish two cases: (i) if $z \in (z_P, z_L]$, L is a monopoly in its local market; (ii) otherwise, if $z \leq z_P$, L competes with firm P for local consumers.

296. In case (i), firm L, which is a monopoly in its area z, chooses a price p_L to maximise

$$w^m(p_L) - c(z), \quad \text{subject to} \quad p_L D^m(p_L) \geq c(z). \tag{13}$$

297. Firm L thus sets the same minimum price $p_L(z) = \underline{p}_L(z)$ as in the monopoly benchmark, such that its budget constraint binds, i.e. $\underline{p}_L(z) D^m\left(\underline{p}_L(z)\right) = c(z)$. In these monopoly areas, L's best response increases with z, but does not depend on z_P and p_P.

298. In case (ii), firm L competes with firm P in its local market, and chooses its price p_L to maximise

$$p_L D_L^d(p_L, p_P) + CS(p_L, p_P) - c(z), \quad \text{subject to} \quad p_L D_L^d(p_L, p_P) \geq c(z). \tag{14}$$

299. Since the objective function is decreasing in p_L,[90] L sets the lowest price such that its budget constraint holds. Therefore, its best-response is given by $p_L^{BR}(p_P, z) = \underline{p}_L^d(p_P, z)$, where $\underline{p}_L^d$ is the solution to

$$\underline{p}_L^d D_L^d\left(\underline{p}_L^d, p_P\right) = c(z). \tag{15}$$

300. Since $D_L^d(p_L, p_P)$ increases with p_P, firm L's best-response $\underline{p}_L^d(p_P, z)$ is decreasing in p_P: when firm P increases its price, firm L reacts by decreasing its own price. Furthermore, L's best response increases with z. The best response exists if L breaks even when it sets its profit-maximising price, $p_L = BR^d(p_P)$.

---

89 The other case, where the private firm leads in investment, is analyzed in Appendix B.2.

90 See the proof of Lemma 4.

301. We now determine firm P's best-response to prices $p_L(z)$ set by the local public firms. Firm P's profit is given by

$$\Pi_P = \int_0^{z_P} p_P D_P^d(p_P, p_L(z))dz - C(z_P). \tag{16}$$

302. Its best-response is then given by the first-order condition

$$\frac{\partial \Pi_P}{\partial p_P} = \int_0^{z_P} \left[p_P \frac{\partial D_P^d}{\partial p_P}(p_P, p_L(z)) + D_P^d(p_P, p_L(z)) \right] dz = 0. \tag{17}$$

303. We assume that there is a unique solution $p_P^{BR}(z_P, p_L(.))$ to this first-order condition, and that the second-order condition,

$$\frac{\partial^2 \Pi_P}{\partial p_P^2} = \int_0^{z_P} \left[2\frac{\partial D_P^d}{\partial p_P}(p_P, p_L(z)) + p_P \frac{\partial^2 D_P^d}{\partial p_P^2}(p_P, p_L(z)) \right] dz \leq 0,$$

304. holds. If demand is linear, P's best-response is the duopoly best-response to the average price set by L in the areas 0 to z_P, as we will see in the linear demand example below.

305. Due to the strategic complementarity assumption, P's best-response $p_P^{BR}(z_P, p_L(.))$ increases if L's prices increase. Furthermore, assuming that $p_L(z)$ is increasing in z (we know that this is true for L's best response), P's best-response increases with z_P, as

$$\left. \frac{\partial^2 \Pi_P}{\partial p_P \partial z_P} \right|_{p_P = p_P^{BR}} = p_P^{BR} \frac{\partial D_P^d}{\partial p_P}\left(p_P^{BR}, p_L(z_P)\right) + D_P^d\left(p_P^{BR}, p_L(z_P)\right) > 0.$$

306. The inequality comes from the fact that due to strategic complementarity, if the first-order condition (FOC) (17) holds, it means that the integrand of (17) is negative for low values of z and positive for high values of z, and thus positive at $z = z_P$. The intuition for the positive relation between p_P^{BR} and z_P is that if $p_L(z)$ is increasing, when P covers costlier areas (with a higher z_P), it faces local firms setting higher prices. P then reacts by increasing its uniform price.

307. **Equilibrium prices.** For given coverage levels, the equilibrium prices P_P and $P_L(z)$ are the solution to (15) and (17). We assume that this solution exists and is uniquely defined.

308. The following proposition characterises how the coverage of the private firm, and hence the overlap between the private firm's and the public firms' networks, affect equilibrium prices.

309. **Proposition 4.** *Assume that the price equilibrium exists, for a given coverage $z_P \leq z_L$. Then, the private firm's equilibrium price P_P increases with z_P, whereas the local public firms prices $P_L(z)$ decrease with z_P. Furthermore, $P_L(z)$ is increasing in z.*

310. *Proof.* Let $\pi_P \equiv p_P D_P^d(p_P, p_L)$ denote P's profit in a local area with prices p_{-P} and p_L. Plugging in L's best response, the first-order condition for firm P can be rewritten as

$$\frac{\partial \Pi_P}{\partial p_P} = \int_0^{z_P} \frac{\partial \pi_P}{\partial p_P}\left(p_P, \underline{p}_L^d(p_P, z)\right)dz \equiv F(p_P, z_P) = 0.$$

311. From the implicit function theorem, we thus have

$$\frac{\partial P_P}{\partial z_P} = -\frac{\partial F / \partial z_P}{\partial F / \partial p_P}.$$

312. Note that we have

$$\frac{\partial F}{\partial p_P} = \int_0^{z_P} \left[\underbrace{\frac{\partial^2 \pi_P}{\partial p_P^2}}_{(-)} + \underbrace{\frac{\partial \pi_P}{\partial p_L}}_{(+)} \underbrace{\frac{\partial \underline{p}_L^d}{\partial p_P}}_{(-)} \right] dz < 0.$$

313. Therefore, $\partial P_P / \partial z_P$ has the sign of $\partial F / \partial z_P$, which we find to be positive:

$$\frac{\partial F}{\partial z_P} = \frac{\partial \pi_P}{\partial p_P}\left(P_P, \underline{p}_L^d(P_P, z_P)\right) > 0,$$

from strategic complementarity and the fact that $\underline{p}_L^d(p_P, z)$ is increasing in z. Therefore, P_P increases with z_P. It follows that $P_L(z)$ decreases with z_P, because $P_L(z)$ gets lower with a higher P_P. Finally, from the definition of $\underline{p}_L^d(p_P, z)$, it is immediate that $P_L(z)$ is increasing in z.

314. This proposition shows that a wider coverage by the private firm has opposite effects on firms' prices. As the private firm covers a larger territory, it faces local public firms that are less aggressive in prices, because they have to charge a higher price to cover their higher investment cost. The private firm thus reacts by increasing its uniform price. By contrast, since the private firm becomes less agressive in its pricing strategy, local public firms react by decreasing their own prices.

315. Note that, while each local firm decreases its price when P expands coverage, the average price of local firms can either decrease or increase with z_P. Let

$$\overline{P}_L \equiv \frac{1}{z_P}\int_0^{z_P} P_L(z)dz = \frac{1}{z_P}\int_0^{z_P} \underline{p}_L^d(P_P, z)dz.$$

316. The variations of the average local price $\overline{P}_L$ with respect to z_P are given by:

$$\frac{\partial \overline{P}_L}{\partial z_P} = \frac{1}{z_P}\left(\underbrace{P_L(z_P) - \overline{P}_L}_{(+)} + \int_0^{z_P} \underbrace{\frac{\partial P_P}{\partial z_P}}_{(+)} \underbrace{\frac{\partial \underline{p}_L^d(P_P, z)}{\partial p_P}}_{(-)} dz \right).$$

317. The first positive term on the right-hand side represents the idea that, when z_P increases, local firms with higher investment costs and, hence, higher prices, enter the duopoly areas, which drives the average local price up. However, this is mitigated by a second, opposite, effect, which is represented by the second term: when z_P increases, firm P increases its price and local firms react by lowering theirs, which tends to reduce the average local price. In the Shubik-Levitan example, we find that the first effect dominates the second one, and hence, the average local price increases with z_P.

6.2. Coverage strategies

318. We now solve for firms P and L's coverage decisions.

319. Since we have assumed that they lead in investment, the local public firms L cover the monopoly areas. Their investment problem in these areas is the same than in the monopoly benchmark: they thus cover up to the area z^m (see Lemma 3).

320. Firm P covers necessarily less than the local public firms. This is because, in the areas covered by local public firms, P faces competition and thus makes less profit than the monopoly profit. P's equilibrium coverage, z^P, if it exists, is therefore lower than $z^L = z^m$.

321. Replacing for P_P and $P_L(z)$, P's profit can be written as

$$\Pi_P = \int_0^{z_P} \pi_P(P_P,P_L(z))dz - C(z_P). \tag{18}$$

322. Using the envelope theorem, P's equilibrium coverage is given by the following first-order condition:

$$\frac{d\Pi_P}{dz_P} = \pi_P(P_P,P_L(z_P)) - c(z_P) = 0$$

323. The two terms represent the direct effect of coverage expansion: P earns an incremental profit in the marginal area, less the investment cost for this area. Let $z^d \equiv \text{argmax}_z zp^d D(p^d,p^d) - C(z)$. We can state the following result:

324. **Proposition 5.** *Assume that the equilibrium to the coverage-price game exists and is unique. In equilibrium,*

(i) The private firm P covers up to $Z_P^l \leq z^d$ and charges the price $P_P^l \leq p^d$;

(ii) The local public firms L cover up to the area $Z_L^l = z^m$. In monopoly areas, they set the same price $P_L^m(z) \leq p^m$ as in the monopoly benchmark. In duopoly areas, they set the price $P_L^l(z)$ such that $P_L^m(z) \leq P_L^l(z) \leq p^d$.

325. *Proof.* Let us first characterise the equilibrium prices. In a given area z, firm L sets the lowest price such that its budget constraint, $p_L D_L^d(p_L,p_P) \geq c(z)$, holds. This price is always lower than the duopoly best-response, $BR^d(p_P)$. Therefore, due to strategic complementarity, in equilibrium firm P will always set a price lower than the duopoly price p^d, and so similarly for firm L (in any area). Finally,

since $D_L^d(p_L,p_P) \leq D^m(p_L)$, in each area z the price set by firm L is higher in the mixed duopoly compared to the monopoly benchmark.

326. Since firms P and L set prices that are lower than the duopoly price, P makes a profit, gross of investment cost, which is lower than the duopoly profit $\pi^d \equiv p^d D^d\left(p^d,p^d\right)$. Its coverage is thus lower than the duopoly coverage $z^d = c^{-1}\left(\pi^d\right)$.

327. The competition between a private firm and local public firms leads to the same total coverage than in the benchmark. This is because local public firms are independent from each other, and in the monopoly areas they thus have the same investment incentives as in the monopoly benchmark.

328. In duopoly areas, prices are lower compared to the benchmark with a monopoly private firm, but higher compared to the benchmark with monopoly local public firms. Indeed, public firms face competition from the private firm, and have to increase their prices in order to break even.

6.3. Linear demand example

329. As an example, we solve for the equilibrium in the linear Shubik-Levitan demand model. To start with, we determine the equilibrium prices for given coverage levels. If it is located in a monopoly area $z \in (z_P,z_L]$, firm L's best-response is given by:

$$p_L(z) = \underline{p}_L(z) = p^m\left(1-\sqrt{1-\frac{c(z)}{\pi^m}}\right),$$

where $\underline{p}_L(z)$ is the lowest price such that the budget constraint holds with a local monopoly.

330. If firm L is located in a duopoly area $z \in [0,z_P]$, its best-response is given by:

$$p_L^{BR}(p_P,z) = \underline{p}_L^d(p_P,z) = BR^d(p_P)\left(1-\sqrt{1-\frac{4c(z)}{(2+\gamma)(BR^d(p_P))^2}}\right).$$

331. Firm P's best-response is given by the first-order condition (17). Since demand is linear, P's best-response to a price scheme $p_L(z)$ set by the local public firms is simply the duopoly best response to the average price set by L in the areas 0 to z_P, that is,

$$p_P = \frac{1}{z_P}\int_0^{z_P} BR^d(p_L(z))dz = BR^d(\overline{p}_L), \tag{19}$$

where $\overline{p}_L = \int_0^{z_P} p_L(z)dz \,/\, z_P$ is the average price set by L in duopoly areas.

332. To solve for the equilibrium prices for given coverage levels, we replace for $\underline{p}_L^d(p_P,z)$ into (19). The equilibrium price P_P then solves

$$P_P = \frac{1}{z_P}\int_0^{z_P} BR^d\left(\underline{p}_L^d(P_P,z)\right)dz = BR^d\left(\overline{p}_L^{BR}(P_P)\right), \tag{20}$$

with $\overline{p}_L^{BR}(P_P) = \int_0^{z_P} \underline{p}_L^d(p_P,z)dz \,/\, z_P$. The equilibrium price for a firm L based in area z is then $P_L(z) = \underline{p}_L^d(P_P,z)$.

333. From (20), we can see that everything is as if firm P were competing with an "average" local public firm, with best response $\overline{p}_L^{BR}(P_P)$. In particular, the equilibrium prices are simply given by the intersection of the duopoly best response $BR^d(\overline{p}_L)$ with the average best response of local firms, $\overline{p}_L^{BR}(p_P)$.

334. Figure 6 shows the equilibrium prices, for given coverage levels, as a function of the private firm's coverage z_P. The investment cost is $c(z) = c_0 z$, with $c_0 = 0.01$, and we set the degree of substituability to $\gamma = 1$. The equilibrium price of the private firm is P_P, whereas $\overline{P}_L$ represents the average price of local firms in the duopoly areas 0 to z_P. For comparison, we show the average price of local firms if they cover the same areas and act as local monopolists, $\overline{P}_L^m$. We see that both P_P and $\overline{P}_L$ increase when the private firm extends coverage. Firm P's price is lower than the duopoly price, while the local firms set higher prices than in a situation where they don't face competition (i.e. $\overline{P}_L > \overline{P}_L^m$).

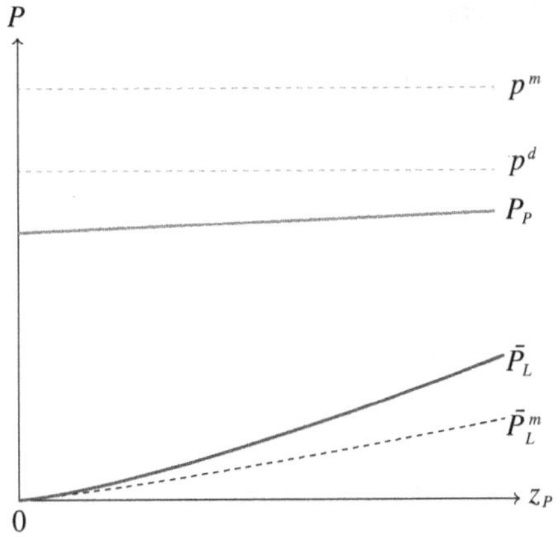

Figure 6 – Variation of prices with respect to z_P

335. We plug in the equilibrium prices for given coverage levels into firm P's profit function, which is given by (18). We then solve for the coverage z_P that maximises P's profit, assuming that $c(z) = c_0 z$. Figure 7 shows the equilibrium prices and coverage levels as a function of the degree of substituability γ, for $c_0 = 0.01$. For the local public firms, we show the average local price in duopoly areas, $\overline{P}_L$. In equilibrium, the private firm and the local public firms set lower prices than the duopoly price p^d, and cover less than the duopoly coverage z^d. As competition intensifies (i.e. γ increases), prices decline and the private firm invests less in coverage.

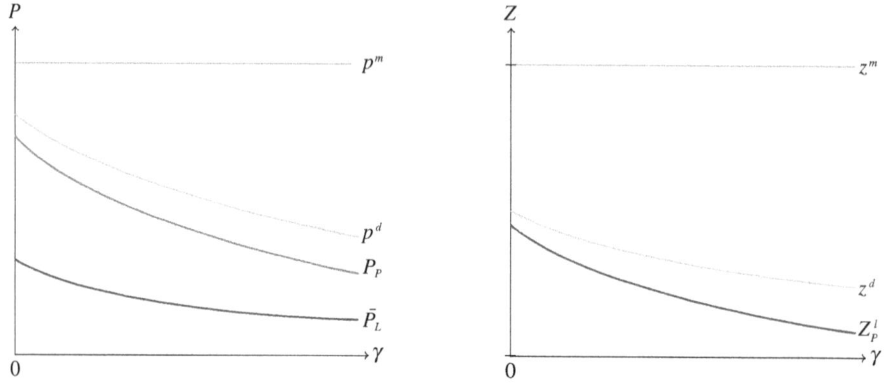

Figure 7 – Equilibrium price and coverage levels if local public firms lead in investment

336. Figure 8 shows the equilibrium welfare level as a function of the degree of substituability γ, for $c_0 = 0.01$. We see that if competition is soft (i.e. low γ), welfare is lower compared to the private monopoly where it is the contrary as competition intensifies.

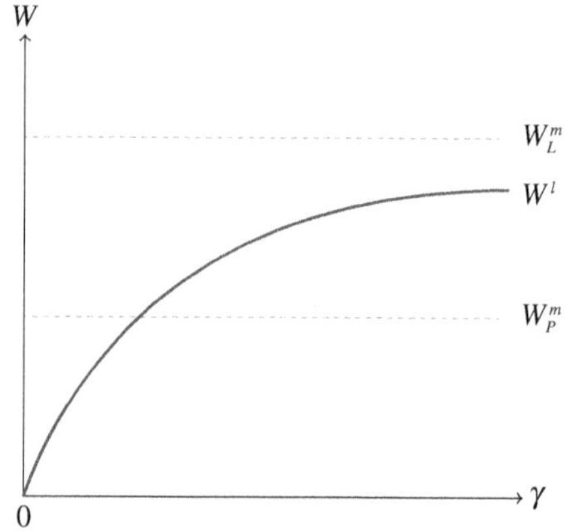

Figure 8 – Equilibrium welfare levels if local public firms lead in investment

7. Conclusion

337. In this paper, we examine a model where a private firm competes with public firms in prices and coverage of a new network infrastructure in a given country. In a monopoly benchmark, we find that the private firm charges the monopoly price and covers up to a monopoly area where the marginal cost of investment is equal to the (local) monopoly profit. A national public firm charges a price lower than the monopoly price, and cross-subsidises between low-cost and high-cost areas, which allows it to cover more than the private firm, that is, up to the area

where the marginal social benefit of investment becomes lower than the marginal cost of investment. Local public firms, which charge prices that are contingent on market conditions in their area, cover the same territory as the private monopoly, but charge lower prices.

338. We then examine a mixed duopoly framework, where the private firm competes with the national public firm or local public firms in prices and coverage and focus on the case where public firms lead in investment, that is, invest more than the private firm in equilibrium. When the private firm competes with the national public firm, we find that the private firm reacts to a price increase of its rival by increasing its own price (strategic complementarity), whereas the national public firm reacts by decreasing its own price (strategic substituability). Moreover, a larger overlap between the private firm's and the public firm's networks drives firms' prices up. We find that, at the equilibrium, total coverage by the national public firm is lower than in the benchmark. Competition leads the private firm to set lower prices than in the benchmark, while the public firm may charge higher prices than in the benchmark. This is due to the competition from the private firm, which makes it harder to sustain low prices.

339. When the private firm competes with local public firms, a larger overlap between the private firm's network and the local public firms' networks leads to a higher price by the private firm and lower prices by the local public firms. When the private firm covers a larger territory, it faces local competitors with higher costs, and therefore it becomes more accommodating. When the private firm increases its price, budget constraints of local public firms are relaxed and they react by decreasing their own prices. We find that, at the equilibrium, total coverage is the same than in the benchmark. The private firm sets a lower price than in the benchmark though, but local public firms set higher prices.

340. Overall, our results suggest that compared to a private monopoly (which may occur in a *grey* area), public investment in a network infrastructure may not always be the most suitable scenario of public intervention. In fact, it depends on the market conditions; it means that a policymaker has to make a complex trade-off between the nature of competition, its intensity, and the costs of network duplication. This also involves the consideration of the opportunity cost of financial public intervention (public investment) compared to regulation.

341. We studied how the competition between a private firm and public firms in prices and coverage of a territory may affect market equilibria. We focussed on firms that are vertically integrated, that is, which operate at both the wholesale and retail levels. The case where public firms operate only upstream, at the wholesale level, also exists. One direction for further research may be to investigate in our framework a scenario where the public firm operates only at the wholesale level, while providing access to competitors at the retail level.

Appendix A
Shubik-Levitan demand model

342. Following Shubik and Levitan (1980), we introduce a representative consumer with the following quasi-linear preferences:

$$U(q_i, q_j, y) = q_i + q_j - \frac{1}{1+\gamma}\left(q_i^2 + q_j^2 + \frac{\gamma}{2}(q_i + q_j)^2\right) + y,$$

where y is the numeraire good and $\gamma \in [0, \infty)$ represents the degree of substitutability between products i and j, a lower γ corresponding to a higher degree of differentiation. If products i and j are both available to the consumer (i.e. we have a duopoly), the demand of firm i is given by:

$$D_i\ (p_i, p_j) = -(2 - (2+\gamma)p_i + \gamma p_j).$$

343. If only one product is available to the consumer, the monopoly demand of firm i is:

$$D^m(p_i) = 1 - p_i.$$

Illustrative model for monopoly benchmark

344. We solve for the equilibrium of the coverage-price game in the linear Shubik-Levitan demand model. We assume that the investment cost in a given area z is $c(z) = z$.

345. **Private firm.** The equilibrium price and coverage of firm P are

$$P_P^m = p^m = 1/2 \quad \text{and} \quad Z_P^m = z^m = c^{-1}\left(p^m D\left(p^m\right)\right) = c^{-1}(1/4) = 1/4.$$

346. Total welfare is $W_P^m = z^m w\left(p^m\right) - C\left(z^m\right) = 1/16.$

347. **National public firm.** For a given coverage z, firm N sets the lowest price such that its budget constraint holds, which is given by

$$\underline{p}_N(z) = p^m\left(1 - \sqrt{1 - \frac{C(z)/z}{\pi^m}}\right).$$

348. Firm N's optimal coverage is then the solution of $w\left(\underline{p}_N(z)\right) = c(z) = z$. We find that firm N's equilibrium coverage is $Z_N^m = 4/9$ and its uniform price is $P_N^m = 1/3$. Total welfare is $W_N^m = Z_N^m w\left(P_N^m\right) - C\left(Z_N^m\right) = 8/81.$

349. **Local public firms.** In a given area z, firm L sets the lowest price such the local budget constraint holds, which is given by

$$\underline{p}_L(z) = p^m\left(1-\sqrt{1-\frac{c(z)}{\pi^m}}\right) = P_L^m(z).$$

350. As shown in Lemma 3, firm L invests if and only if $z \leq z^m = Z_L^m$. Total welfare is $W_L^m = \int_0^{z^m}\left(w\left(\underline{p}_L(z)\right) - c(z)\right)dz = 17/192$.

Appendix B
The private firm leads in investment

351. In this appendix, we briefly analyse the case where the private firm has invested more than the national public firm (Appendix B.1), and where it has invested more than the local public firms (Appendix B.2).

Appendix B.1
National public firm vs private firm

Pricing strategies

352. We start by determining the equilibrium prices of firms *P* and *N* for given coverage levels z_N and z_P , with $z_P > z_N$.

353. **Best responses.** Consider first the pricing decision of the private firm. *P* chooses a price p_P to maximise its profit, which is given by

$$\Pi_P = (z_P - z_N) p_P D^m(p_P) + z_N p_P D_P^d(p_P, p_N) - C(z_P), \tag{21}$$

354. Firm *P*'s best-response is given by

$$\frac{z_N}{z_P} \frac{\partial\left[pD_P^d(p, p_N)\right]}{\partial p} + \left(1 - \frac{z_N}{z_P}\right) \frac{\partial\left[pD^m(p)\right]}{\partial p} = 0. \tag{22}$$

355. From the above equation , we observe that if $z_N = 0$, firm *P*'s best-reponse is the monopoly price, p^m, whereas if $z_N \to z_P$, its best-response is close to the duopoly best-response, $BR^d(p_N)$. Therefore, *P*'s best-response to a price p_N, is $p_P^{BR}(p_N, z_N, z_P) \in \left(BR^d(p_N), p^m\right)$.

356. Consider now the public firm's pricing decision of the public firm. Firm *N* chooses its price p_N to maximise its objective function, which is given by

$$\Pi_N = z_N\left(p_N D_N^d(p_P, p_N) + CS(p_P, p_N)\right) - C(z_N), \tag{23}$$

subject to the budget constraint

$$z_N p_N D_N^d(p_P, p_N) \geq C(z_N). \tag{24}$$

357. Proceeding in a similar way than as in Lemma 4, *N*'s best-response to a price p_P is to set the lowest price such that its budget constraint (24) binds, that

is, $p_N^{BR}(p_P) = \underline{p}_N^d(p_P, z_N)$, where $\underline{p}_N^d$ satisfies $z_N \underline{p}_N^d D_N^d(\underline{p}_N^d, p_P) = C(z_N)$. This price is lower than or equal to the uniform price that maximises its total profit (i.e. $\hat{p}_N = BR^d(p_N)$). If at the profit-maximising price $\hat{p}_N$, firm *N* does not break even, there is no best-response to the price set by the private firm.

358. Proceeding in a similar way as in Lemma 5, prices are strategic complements for firm *P* and strategic substitutes for firm *N*.

359. **Equilibrium prices.** The equilibrium prices P_P and P_N are given by the intersection of the best responses of the private firm and the public firm. We assume that this intersection exists. To study how coverage affects pricing decisions, we define the ratio of coverage levels $\delta \equiv z_N / z_P \in (0,1)$. The equilibrium prices can then be written as functions of z_N and δ: $P_P = P_P(z_N, \delta)$ and $P_N = P_N(z_N, \delta)$.

360. The following proposition characterises how the coverage by firm *P* and the degree of overlap ($\delta = z_N / z_P$) between firm *P*'s and firm *N*'s networks affect equilibrium prices.

361. **Result 1.** *Assume that the price equilibrium exists, for given coverage levels.*

- *For a given coverage z_N by the national public firm, firm N's equilibrium price P_N decreases with z_P, whereas firm P's equilibrium price increases with z_P.*
- *For given coverage z_P by the private firm, $\partial P_N / \partial \delta \gtreqless 0$ and $\partial P_P / \partial \delta < 0$ if and only if $P_N D^d(P_N, P_P) \geq c(z_N)$ while $\partial P_N / \partial \delta > 0$ and $\partial P_P / \partial \delta \gtreqless 0$ if and only if $P_N D^d(P_N, P_P) \leq c(z_N)$.*

Coverage strategies

362. We now consider the coverage decisions of firms *N* and *P*, for given prices p_N and p_P. From (21) and (23), the equilibrium coverage levels are solutions to the system of first-order conditions,

$$p_P D_P^m(p_P) = c(z_P),$$
$$p_N D_N^d(p_N, p_P) + CS(p_N, p_P) = c(z_N),$$

363. Replacing for $p_N = P_N(z_P, z_N)$ and $p_P = P_P(z_P, z_N)$, the equilibrium coverage of firms *N* and *P* are the solution of

$$P_P(z_P, z_N) D_P^m(P_P(z_P, z_N)) = c(z_P), \quad (25)$$

$$P_N(z_P, z_N) D_N^d(P_N(z_P, z_N), P_P(z_P, z_N)) + CS(P_N(z_P, z_N), P_P(z_P, z_N)) = c(z_N). \quad (26)$$

364. **Result 2.** *Assume that the equilibrium to the coverage-price game exists and is unique. In equilibrium,*

(i) The private firm P covers a smaller territory than in the benchmark and charges a lower price, that is, $Z_P^n < Z_P^m$ and $P_P^n < P_P^m$.

(ii) The public firm N covers a smaller territory than in the benchmark and charges a lower price, that is, $Z_N^n < Z_N^m$ and $P_N^n < P_P^m$.

Appendix B.2 Private vs local public firms

Pricing strategies

365. We analyse firms' pricing strategies for given coverage levels z_P and z_L, with $z_P \geq z_L$.

366. **Best responses.** Consider first the pricing decision of a local public firm L based in a given area $z \leq z_L$. As in Section 6.1 (case (ii)), L competes with P in its local market, and chooses its price p_L to maximise

$$p_L D_L^d(p_L, p_P) + CS(p_L, p_P) - c(z), \quad \text{subject to} \quad p_L D_L^d(p_L, p_P) \geq c(z). \quad (27)$$

367. Firm L's best-response is then $p_L^{BR}(p_P, z) = \underline{p}_L^d(p_P, z)$, where $\underline{p}_L^d$ is the solution to (15).

368. We find that when P increases its price, L reacts by decreasing its own price and that L's best response increases with z. The best response exists if L breaks even when it sets its profit-maximising price, $p_L = BR^d(p_P)$.

369. We now determine firm P's best-response to prices $p_L(z)$ set by the local public firms. Firm P's profit is given by

$$\Pi_P = \int_0^{z_L} p_P D_P^d(p_P, p_L(z))dz + \int_{z_L}^{z_P} p_P D_P^m(p_P)dz - C(z_P). \quad (28)$$

370. Its best-response is given by the first-order condition

$$\frac{\partial \Pi_P}{\partial p_P} = \int_0^{z_L}\left[p_P \frac{\partial D_P^d}{\partial p_P}(p_P, p_L(z)) + D_P^d(p_P, p_L(z))\right]dz$$
$$+(z_P - z_L)\left[p_P \frac{\partial D_P^m}{\partial p_P}(p_P) + D_P^m(p_P)\right] = 0. \quad (29)$$

371. We assume that there is a unique solution $p_P^{BR}(z_L, z_P, p_L(.))$ to this first-order condition, and that the second-order condition,

$$\frac{\partial^2 \Pi_P}{\partial p_P^2} = \int_0^{z_L}\left[2\frac{\partial D_P^d}{\partial p_P}(p_P, p_L(z)) + p_P \frac{\partial^2 D_P^d}{\partial p_P^2}(p_P, p_L(z))\right]dz$$
$$+(z_P - z_L)\left[2\frac{\partial D_P^m}{\partial p_P}(p_P) + p_P \frac{\partial^2 D_P^m}{\partial p_P^2}(p_P)\right] \leq 0,$$

holds.

372. Due to the strategic complementarity assumption, P's best-response $p_P^{BR}(z_L,z_P,p_L(.))$ increases if L's prices increase. Furthermore, assuming that $p_L(z)$ is increasing in z, P's best-response increases with z_P, as

$$\left.\frac{\partial^2 \Pi_P}{\partial p_P \partial z_P}\right|_{p_P=p_P^{BR}} = p_P^{BR}\frac{\partial D_P^m}{\partial p_P}\left(p_P^{BR}\right) + D_P^m\left(p_P^{BR}\right) > 0.$$

373. Firm P's best-response p_P^{BR} increases with z_P as covering more increases the investment cost of P, thereby increasing P's uniform price.

374. Firm P's best-response price decreases with z_L as

$$\left.\frac{\partial^2 \Pi_P}{\partial p_P \partial z_L}\right|_{p_P=p_P^{BR}} = p_P^{BR}\frac{\partial D_P^d}{\partial p_P}(p_P,p_L(z_L)) + D_P^d(p_P,p_L(z_L))$$

$$-\left(p_P^{BR}\frac{\partial D_P^m}{\partial p_P}\left(p_P^{BR}\right) + D_P^m\left(p_P^{BR}\right)\right) < 0.$$

375. As z_L increases, the investment cost of local public firms covering (the new areas) increases. If $p_L(z)$ is increasing, firm P faces local public firms setting higher prices and thus reacts by increasing its uniform price (first two terms on the right). On the other hand, a higher z_L means that P benefits less from monopoly areas and faces competition from local public firms, affecting negatively its price (last two terms on the right).

376. **Equilibrium prices.** The equilibrium prices $P_P(z_L,z_P)$ and $P_L(z,z_L,z_P)$ are the solution to (15) and (29). We assume that this solution exists and is uniquely defined.

377. The following proposition characterises how the coverage of the private firm, and hence the overlap between the private firm's and the public firms' networks, affect equilibrium prices.

378. **Result 3.** *Assume that the price equilibrium exists, for a given coverage* $z_L \leq z_P$. *Then, the private firm's equilibrium price* P_P *increases (decreases) with* z_P (z_L)*, whereas the local public firms prices* $P_L(z)$ *decrease (increase) with* z_P (z_L)*. Furthermore,* $P_L(z)$ *is increasing in* z.

Coverage strategies

379. We now solve for firms P and L's coverage decisions. Replacing for $P_P(z_L,z_P)$ and $P_L(z,z_L,z_P)$, P's profit is given by

$$\Pi_P = \int_0^{z_L} \pi_P^d(P_P,P_L(z))dz + \int_{z_L}^{z_P} \pi_P^m(P_P)dz - C(z_P).$$

380. Using the envelope theorem, P's equilibrium coverage is given by the following first-order condition:

$$\frac{d\Pi_P}{dz_P} = \pi_P^m(P_P) - c(z_P)$$

381. The two terms on the right hand side represent the direct effect of coverage expansion: P earns an incremental profit in the marginal (monopoly) area, less the investment cost for this area. We now state the following result:

382. **Result 4.** *Assume that the equilibrium to the coverage-price game exists and is unique. In equilibrium,*

(i) The private firm P covers up to $Z_P^l < Z_P^m = z^m$ *and charges the price* $P_P^l < p^m$;

(ii) The local public firms cover up to $Z_L^l < Z_L^m = z^m$. *They set the price* $P_L^l(z)$ *such that* $P_L^m(z) \leq P_L^l(z) < p^m$.

Chapter 3
Privacy, Competition and Multi-Homing

1. Introduction

383. Markets are affected by digital transformation by which business and competencies evolve in order to fully leverage opportunities of digital technologies. This leads to the consideration of digital markets, where firms (or platforms) compete in an economic environment mainly characterised by markets that are multi-sided, the existence of network effects, and the collection and use of consumer information. Prominent examples are the social network Facebook and the operating system of Google, Android. A digital market is multi-sided if an intermediary economic platform has two or more distinct user groups that provide network benefits to each other. The collection and use of consumer information stems from firms that collects data from the users signing up to their services. Consumer information can be monetised; for instance, a firm can sell consumer information to advertisers so that they better target consumers, but also to data brokers, or even use it to improve its own services.

384. As a result, competition authorities face new issues in enforcing competitive rules. Indeed, digital firms compete in prices but also in privacy, which is related to the way consumer information is exploited by firms, that is, on the disclosure of consumer information in data markets. Consumers care about their privacy and may not be willing to provide personal information if firms monetise it, even if this is in exchange of improved services. Competition as well as data protection authorities therefore face a trade-off between allowing firms to exploit more consumer information to improve services and consumer privacy concerns.[91]

385. A striking example is the Facebook/WhatsApp (2014) merger, which has been subject to intense debate about the firms' incentives to merge and the impact of this merger on consumer welfare. At the time of the merger (3 October 2014), Facebook had 1.3 billion users, while WhatsApp had 600 million users. The European Commission (EC) assessed the impact of the transaction on three services: consumer communications, social networking, and online (non-search) advertising. The EC concluded that firms were distant competitors in markets

---

91 Note that increased privacy concerns could arise from the concentration (of the collection and use) of data, for instance, after a merger. See *ibid.* note 34.

for consumer communications and social networking, and that, post merger, both consumers and advertisers would continue to have a large choice of alternatives (i.e. communications and online advertising services). The merger was approved even considering the possibility of automated user matching, since a large amount of valuable consumer information would continue to exist. In addition, Facebook said that it was not technically possible to match WhatsApp users' ID with Facebook accounts.[92] However, in August 2016, WhatsApp annouced it would start disclosing its users' phone numbers and analytics data about its users to Facebook. On 18 May 2017, Facebook was fined 110m by the European Union for providing misleading information on the technical impossibility of matching users of both platforms. The European Consumer Organisation (BEUC) announced it was disappointing that the Commission had not revised its original decision in favour of the merger. The BEUC director general, Monique Goyens said:[93]

> It is crucial in our data economy that competition bodies more closely scrutinise the potential consumer harm of a merger between data-heavy companies. The commission failed to do so when it gave the go-ahead to the Facebook-WhatsApp takeover.

386. The Bundeskartellamt (German cartel office) has also investigated whether Facebook is abusing its dominant position by failing to inform people about how their personal data is being used.[94] On February 7, 2019, the Bundeskartellamt decided to prohibit Facebook from combining user data from different sources.[95]

387. Privacy concerns therefore raise the question of how firms integrate information disclosure in their business strategies and how this affects competition. In this respect, one can observe the emergence of business models that suggest a trade-off between consumer privacy and the exploitation of consumer information. For instance, Google supplies consumers with various digital services, for example, mail (Gmail), photo storage (Google Photos), maps (Google Maps, Waze), at a zero price. Meanwhile, it collects and use personal information provided by users; it does so by profiling consumers and charging advertisers to target them. Google's business model is therefore essentially data-driven, with low or even zero prices and low privacy. In the same vein, since 2016, Facebook has been subsidising

---

92 The reason given was that most users did not load their phone number used to register on WhatsApp onto their Facebook profile. However, in August 2016, WhatsApp announced updates to its terms of services and privacy policy with the possibility of linking a WhatsApp user phone number with Facebook user identities. See EC press release on 18 May 2017. http://europa.eu/rapid/press-release_IP-17-1369_en.htm

93 See *The Guardian, 18 May 2017.* https://www.theguardian.com/business/2017/may/18/facebook-fined-eu-whatsapp-european-commission

94 Note that as of 15 May 2021, WhatsApp privacy policy has evolved: the new terms allow Facebook and WhatsApp to share payment and transaction data for better targeted advertising. Moreover, Facebook is looking to merge its messaging plateforms (Messenger and WhatsApp). See *TechCrunch, 19 February 2021.* https://techcrunch.com/2021/02/19/whatsapp-details-what-will-happen-to-users-who-dont-agree-to-privacy-changes/?guccounter=1 guce_referrer=aHR0cHM6Ly93d3cuZ29vZ2xlLmNvbS8 guce_referrer_sig=AQAAAKaLF0CQLxdt-zW-rV4b_LF8DkvoKvN58nfK0rhCNrDR-gFFhU_OwghOkRoTB6ll73x6MhwOWFZXCD9K3mVNIP-jCEyzwT0LKo8yFx-37M-Sp0FQuLGY1RwY1iMvI3eal-NuVJEQHFF2Hkwq-x7FkUkV19bGPrR2zj76nY-B3Y2C

95 See Bundeskartellamt's decision on 7 February 2019. https://www.bundeskartellamt.de/SharedDocs/Publikation/EN/Pressemitteilungen/2019/07_02_2019_Facebook_FAQs.pdf?__blob=publicationFile v=5

(i.e. negative pricing) some users up to $20 per month to sell their privacy by installing the iOS or Android "Facebook Research" app.[96] By contrast, Apple has adopted a different business model. It charges for digital services, for instance, data storage (iCloud) or music (Apple Music), bundled with Apple products (iPad, iPhone etc.). Also, Apple has a strict privacy policy and does not exploit consumer information.[97] This policy is a central aspect of Apple's brand image.[98] Its business model is therefore driven by purchase revenues and a high level of privacy. The same applies for Microsoft, which has introduced Office 365, an online service that competes with Google's by allowing consumers to edit documents, manage email, contacts, and calendar events. Microsoft charges consumers for the service and does not disclose their information for advertising purposes.

388. These examples highlight the different business strategies that digital firms may employ regarding consumer information. That said, these strategies may be affected by consumer purchase behaviour. Indeed, when firms (or platforms) provide a service, consumers may sign-up to not only one service (single-homing) but to several services (multi-homing). A consumer may buy different variants of horizontally differentiated services, depending on the extent to which service functionalities are overlapping (e.g. Google's search engine vs Bing's, Netflix vs Amazon Prime Video).

389. Competition in digital markets therefore raiseq the issue of new business models in relation to privacy and consumer purchase behavior. In this chapter, we examine the impact of competition between firms in prices and information disclosure levels. We build a two-sided market model where two firms supply a horizontally differentiated service to consumers on one side, and sell consumer information to a monopoly data broker on the other side.[99] Consumers observe the level of disclosure in which firms engage and their price before deciding which service to patronise and how much personal information to provide. The perceived quality of the firm's service for each consumer increases with information provision and decreases with the firm's level of disclosure. Firms derive revenue from two sources: purchase revenues from the prices charged to consumers, and information disclosure revenues from the collection and use of consumer information. The latter depend on the firm's disclosure level, the stock of consumer information, and the selling price of this information to the data broker.[100]

---

96 Due to privacy issues, Apple removed (August 2018) the application Onavo Protect through which Facebook was collecting a huge amount of data. Facebook sidestepped the App Store and rewarded users who downloaded Facebook Research, which gave it root access to network traffic in what may be a violation of Apple policy. Apple subsequently blocked this application. In a similar, way, Apple removed the application Screewise Meter from Google. See *TechCrunch, 30 January 2019.* https://techcrunch.com/2019/01/30/apple-bans-facebook-vpn/

97 However, Apple distributes a number of applications for which exploitation of data is the economic model. See *Les Echos, 22 March 2019.* https://www.lesechos.fr/tech-medias/hightech/donnees-privees-apple-est-il-vraiment-le-bon-eleve-1002692

98 See Apple's App Tracking Transparency, introduced in April 2021, through which "users will be able to see which apps have requested permission to track, and make changes as they see fit". https://developer.apple.com/documentation/apptrackingtransparency

99 As in Anderson, Foros, and Kind (2019), we call this framework "two-sided" in that firms (platforms) can derive revenues not only from the demand side (consumers) but also from the supply side (data broker).

100 This framework is related to that of Casadesus-Masanell and Hervas-Drane (2015).

390. We first examine this framework in a benchmark where consumers can only single-home (i.e. sign-up to only one service). We find that firms adopt two types of business strategies captured by a trade-off between the collection and use of consumer information, the level of information provision, and consumer valuations. If consumer valuations are sufficiently low, firms engage in disclosure of consumer information (low-privacy regime): the lower consumer valuations are, the more firms exploit consumer information, but the lower the level of information provision. Firms can even subsidise consumers (negative pricing) if their valuations are very low or if competition intensity (captured by the parameter of the transportation cost) is high in the market. Firms represent a bottleneck for access to consumer information and charge the data broker the monopoly price, leaving her with zero surplus. In other words, firms adopt a data-driven business model.

391. On the other hand, if consumer valuations are sufficiently high, firms do not engage in disclosure of consumer information (high-privacy regime) and always charge positive prices. Firms thus adopt a purchase-driven business model where they do not rely on disclosure revenues.

392. We then examine the case of multi-product monopoly and find qualitatively the same intuitions. We show that a merger to monopoly is profitable for firms because it increases market power. A merger, that has no impact on privacy, harms consumers.

393. We then consider the possibility that some consumers multi-home (i.e. sign-up to both services). Multi-Homing depends on the incremental value of signing up to a second service. We find that firms' business strategies involve a trade-off between the collection and use of consumer information, the level of information provision, and consumer valuation, as in the single-homing benchmark. However, we show that this trade-off is affected by the incentives to multi-home, the ability of firms to monetise multi-homing consumer information, and competition intensity. In particular, we distinguish between two cases: one where multi-homing consumer information is homogenous (i.e. firms sell the same information to the data broker), and another one where it is differentiated (i.e. firms sell different information to the data broker).

394. We find that, for given multi-homing incentives and competition intensity, if consumer valuations are sufficiently high and provided, firms do not rely on the exploitation of consumer information at all, and as in the single-homing benchmark, their business model is purchase-driven. In this case, the attributes of multi-homing consumer information does not affect firms' business strategies. A merger to monopoly is welfare-neutral in that it has no effect, neither on prices nor on privacy.

395. In contrast, if consumer valuations are sufficiently low (and for given multi-homing incentives and competition intensity), the attributes of multi-homing consumer information affects firms' decisions. When multi-homer information is homogenous, firms are unable to monetise it, as they sell twice the same information to the data broker and Bertrand competition brings the price of data to zero for these consumers. They generate disclosure revenues from the information of single-homers only and the surplus of the data broker increases as there are more multi-homers. Firms do not resort to consumer subsidisation and obtain lower profits as consumers have more incentives to multi-home, even if this negative effect is less pronounced when competition intensity is low. We show that a merger

to monopoly mitigates the issue of the monetisation of multi-homer information. We find that in this case, a merger, which decreases prices and privacy levels, harms consumers.

396. When multi-homing consumer information is differentiated, firms are competitive bottlenecks on all consumer information; they can thus fully monetise the information provided by multi-homers. In this case, for given multi-homing incentives and competition intensity, we retrieve the trade-off of the single-homing benchmark between the firm's disclosure level and the level of information provision. If consumer valuations are very low, firms resort to consumer subsidisation in exchange for exploiting more consumer information. A merger to monopoly has no effect, neither on prices nor on the way consumer information is exploited. Apart from monopolising the market, firms have no incentive to merge in this case.

397. Section 2 discusses the related literature. Section 3 presents the model framework. In Section 4, we solve for firms' decisions when consumers can only single-home. In Section 5, we examine the case where multi-homing is possible. Section 6 concludes. All proofs are in the appendix.

2. Relation to literature

398. This chapter is related to the literature on the economics of privacy.

399. The seminal papers on privacy are those by Stigler (1980) and Posner (1981); these authors argue that privacy could lead to allocation inefficiencies by allowing individuals to hide some characteristics; privacy is therefore undesirable in the absence of externalities or explicit preferences for privacy. Hermalin and Katz (2006) challenge this view. They examine the impact of different privacy regimes on allocative efficiency absent externalities and preferences. They find that more privacy may be efficient in some cases. Calzolari and Pavan (2006) consider information disclosure between two firms (principals) that are interested in discovering consumers' willingness to pay. In a model of sequential contracting, a common agent strategically decides whether to report her true type. Calzolari and Pavan find that the transmission of personal data from one company to another may in some cases reduce information distortions and enhance social welfare. In a survey on the economics of privacy, Hui and Png (2006) show that externalities generally play an important role in the collection and use of consumer information.[101]

400. Firms collect and use consumer information in various ways, such as in advertising. Tag (2009) examines a monopoly platform that offers either an ad-free pure subscription option or an ad-only program to discriminate consumers. The author shows that the subscription option induces a higher level of advertising for those remaining on the ad-only option. He finds that aggregate consumer surplus falls, whereas the advertiser surplus rises through lower ad prices. In an extended framework where

101 See also Acquisti, Taylor and Wagman (2016), for a comprehensive literature review on the economics of privacy.

consumers can choose a costly ad-avoidance technology, Anderson and Gans (2011) confirm the result of Tag (2009). De Cornière and Nijs (2016) examine firms' bidding strategies in auctions for more precise targeting of their advertisements. The idea is that consumer information provides a better segmentation of the population. By disclosing information about consumers, the platform ensures that consumers will see the most relevant advertisements, whereas when no information is disclosed under a complete privacy regime, ads are displayed randomly. The authors find that targeted advertising can lead to higher prices and that improving match quality by disclosing consumer information to firms might be too costly to an intermediary because of the informational rent that is passed on to firms. Given a relationship between the match quality of advertising and consumer demand, de Cornière and Nijs (2016) show that it is possible to specify conditions under which some privacy or some limits to disclosure are optimal for an intermediary.

401. Consumers have privacy concerns about their personal information and this impacts competition. Noam (1995a, 1995b) discusses the privacy implications of advances in telecommunications and argues that a competitive marketplace can contribute solutions to consumer demands for privacy. In the same vein, Spulber (2009) establishes that competition in online search and advertising market can drive search firms' decisions towards more privacy and increase consumer surplus. Casadesus-Masanell and Hervas-Drane (2015) analyze the effect of competition on consumer privacy. They examine a model where firms compete in privacy (i.e. information disclosure levels). Consumers provide voluntarily personal information to firms in order to obtain higher-quality products. Firms can disclose and sell some of this information to an outside firm, which negatively impacts consumers' utility. The authors determine that the market equilibrium involves vertical differentiation with respect to disclosure of consumers' information. One firm positions itself as a high-quality (low-disclosure) provider, and the other firm as a low-quality (high-disclosure) provider. Moerover, they show that more intense competition implies more disclosure by the firms, which implies that stronger market power does not necessarily imply that firms disclose more information about their users. In other words, more intense competition between firms reduce consumer privacy, which can be compensated by consumer subsidisation. The policy implication of Casadesus-Masanell and Hervas-Drane' framework is that one should expect low level of privacy in a competitive marketplace but this does not necessarily harm consumer welfare.[102]

402. Montes, Sand-Zantman and Valletti (2018) study a framework with endogenous privacy, where two firms obtain data from a data broker. They show that in equilibrium the data broker sells its data to only one firm, and therefore only one of the competing firms can set personalised prices.[103] The firm that has access to the data makes more

[102] Lefouili and Toh (2018) study the impact of privacy regulation on quality. A monopolist supplies its service for free and derives revenues from information disclosure. Consumes choose whether to use the service and how much information to provide. They show, among other results, that in a fully covered market, a disclosure cap decreases quality but is socially desirable in some cases.

[103] Dosis and Sand-Zantman (2021) study the effects of property rights over the use of data on market outcomes. The authors show that both the firm and users prefer the users (the firm) to own the rights for low (high) values of data.

profit than if it were without information about consumers, and the firm without access to data makes a lower profit. In this case, a move from uniform to personalised prices decreases total welfare, though consumers benefit from this move.[104]

403. Collection and use of consumer information affects firms' decisions in the market (e.g. mergers, investments). In a dynamic model of R&D competition, Prufer and Schottmuller (2021) examine competition in data-driven markets, that is, markets where the cost of quality is decreasing in the amount of machine-generated data about user preferences or characteristics. In every period, duopolistic competitors repeatedly choose their rates of innovation, that is, firms can increment the quality of their product. The cost of providing an arbitrary incremental quality is decreasing as the firm's market share increases. Their model incorporates "data-driven indirect network effects" (similar to learning effects) that arise on the supply side of a market via decreasing marginal costs of innovation, but are driven by user demand. Consumer information is collected by the firm that uses it to adapt the product better to users' preferences, thereby increasing perceived quality in the future. They show that data-driven markets become stable monopolies and that in a tipped market, innovation incentives both for the dominant firm (incumbent) and for competitors are small. First, the relatively lower innovation cost induces the incumbent to invest less. In addition, the disadvantaged entrant has an incentive to disengage. Prufer and Schottmuller (2021) also find that incumbents with a dominant position can leverage their market power to conquer "connected markets", that is, markets in which the same user data allows an improved quality at a lower marginal cost. This data-driven "domino effect" may explain why web giants are increasingly invading markets, often seemingly unrelated to their core business.

404. Prat and Valletti (2019) study digital platforms as attention brokers that have proprietary information about their users' product preferences and sell targeted ad space to retail product industries. Retail producers compete for access to this attention bottleneck. The authors define attention brokersby their ability to obtain information about the preferences of individual users and to target ads to them. They show that increased concentration among attention brokers may lead to reduced entry in retail product industries (through higher prices and less product variety), which ends up harming consumer welfare. They argue that a monopolistic attention broker has an incentive to create an attention bottleneck by reducing the supply of targeted advertising. If fewer ads are sold, this will reduce the number of retail firms that have access to consumers, thus increasing (attention brokers') market power. This translates into higher total profits for the retail industry, partially captured by the platform through higher total ad revenue. The authors finally show that a merger between platforms can increase market power in the retail industry to the detriment of consumers.

405. This chapter paper is also related to the seminal literature on two-sided markets (Rochet and Tirole, 2003; Caillaud and Jullien, 2003; Armstrong, 2006). Armstrong (2006) shows that in a two-sided market with cross-group network effects

104 In the public economics literature, Choi, Jeon and Kim (2019) show that the market equilibrium level of privacy may still be too low relative to the social optimum.

(e.g. the benefit of joining the platform on one side depends on the size of the group joining the platform on the other side), equilibrium prices are determined by (i) the magnitude of the cross-group network effects, (ii) whether fees are levied on a lump-sum or per-transaction basis, and (iii) whether agents single or multi-home.

406. Choi (2010) analyzes the effect of tying a two-sided market where agents can multi-home. He shows that tying is associated with more multi-homing on the consumer side and that it also benefits content providers as platform-specific exclusive content is available to more consumers. Tying can therefore be welfare-improving if multi-homing is allowed. Belleflamme and Peitz (2019) evaluate how platforms, buyers, and sellers are affected when (non-competing) sellers are able to multi-home. They show that the common wisdom according to which platforms and buyers should benefit from this possibility, but sellers should not, is not always correct. In fact, platforms may prefer to prevent sellers from multi-homing and this would then hurt buyers; the authors conjecture that this is more likely to happen in environments with competing sellers. One reason for this is that competing sellers are more willing to accept exclusivity agreements, which increases coordination, thereby relaxing competition among them. The authors find that it would make exclusive agreements more profitable for platforms (as sellers are more willing to accept them) and even less desirable for buyers (by paying higher fees to platforms and by facing fewer sellers with more market power). Belleflamme and Peitz conclude that these results are important for antitrust authorities that examine whether exclusivity agreements between platforms and sellers should be allowed or not.

407. Anderson, Foros, and Kind (2019) study the impact of consumer multi-homing on market equilibrium and performance. They adopt a circular model of product differentiation, where platforms may charge both sides of the market, that is, consumers and advertisers. The authors show that equilibrium consumer prices are independent of the number of platforms when some but not all consumers multi-home. On the contrary, advertising prices decrease as the fraction of multi-homers increases. Moreover, a merger between two platforms does not affect consumer prices, but is profitable since the merging platforms can charge advertisers. The authors also show that an incumbent may have less incentive than an entrant to set up an additional platform. They conclude that compared to single-homing, multi-homing flips the side of the market on which platforms compete and that equilibrium product variety can be insufficient under multihoming.

408. In a companion paper, Anderson, Foros and Kind (2017) examine in a one-sided market the characteristics of single-homing and multi-homing equilibrium. The authors assume that each product has its own specific part, while there also exists a common overlapping part that belongs to both products. Each firm can make its product exclusive (in other words, its opponent doesn't have the product), and hence the customers can consume only one of the products (single-home) rather than both (multi-home). Without product overlap, allowing multi-homing should be better for the firms because they have greater demand and less fierce competition. With overlap, each firm cannot charge for the common part, as they compete à la Bertrand. Therefore, allowing multi-homing could make the firms worse-off because of overlap and horizontal differentiation.

3. Model

409. We study a two-sided market where firms compete in prices and information disclosure levels. Two firms, A and B, are located on a Hotelling line and supply a service to consumers at zero marginal cost. The firms are located at the two extremes of a line of length 1, with firm A located at point 0 and firm B at point 1. Consumers are uniformly distributed along the line, and choose to sign up for a service from firm A, firm B, or both if this is possible.

410. A consumer purchasing only the service of firm $i = A,B$ (single-homing) decides on the level of personal information $y_i \in [0,1]$ to provide to this firm.[105] The net utility of the consumer, located at $x \in [0,1]$, when purchasing service i, for given price p_i and information disclosure $d_i \in [0,1]$, is

$$U_i = vy_i^{1/2}\left(2 - y_i^{1/2} - d_i y_i^{1/2}\right) - p_i - tx_i, \tag{1}$$

where $v > 0$ is a parameter that reflects the intrinsic benefit of the service, and $tx_i = tx$ is the transportation cost incurred when buying for firm $i = A$ and $tx_i = t(1-x)$ the transportation cost when buying from firm $i = B$.[106]

411. The term $y_i^{1/2}\left(2 - y_i^{1/2} - d_i y_i^{1/2}\right)$ in equation (1) represents the quality of firm i's service. This specification implies that quality is concave in the level of information provision y_i. This means that consumers benefit from providing information, because it enables the firm to provide a personalised, higher quality service; but at the margin, this benefit is decreasing. Moreover, the informational quality is decreasing in the level of information disclosure d_i, meaning that consumers incur disutility from information disclosure.

412. Firm i decides on a price $p_i \in \mathbb{R}$ and a disclosure level $d_i \in [0,1]$. Firms derive revenues from purchases but also thay can set negative prices (i.e. to subsidise consumers). Firms can also derive revenues by disclosing consumer information on a data market. More precisely, firm i sells consumer information to a monopoly data broker, at a price r_i per user and piece of information. This means that firm i's revenue from selling the information of one user is $d_i y_i \times r_i$. Let $D_i(.)$ be the demand of firm i. The profit of firm i is then

$$\Pi_i = (p_i + d_i y_i r_i) D_i.$$

413. We now characterise the utility of buying consumer information for the data broker. Let $v^b > 0$ be the value placed by the data broker on the information of each user signing up to service i. When acquiring firm i's consumer information, the net utility of the data broker is thus given by $\left(v^b - r_i\right)D_i$.

---

105 The framework where a consumer can purchase both services (multi-homing) is presented later in Section 5.

106 Our utility function is different from that of Casadesus-Masanell and Hervas-Drane (2015), where the authors examine a model of vertical differentiation with single-homing. Using their formulation in our model, we would obtain untractable solutions (in most cases) when allowing for multi-homing. In the Appendix, we briefly derive their framework with single-homing and horizontal differentiation.

414. We consider the following sequence of events. At the first stage, firms simultaneously set their disclosure level d_i.[107] At the second stage, firms simultaneously set their price p_i and determine the selling price r_i of consumer information. At the third stage, having observed prices and disclosure levels, consumers choose to purchase firm A's or firm B's service, or to stay out of the market. At the fourth stage, consumers decide on the level of information provision y_i to the firm i they have patronised.

415. We look for the subgame perfect equilibrium of this game.

4. Single-homing

416. We start by considering single-homing, that is, a situation where consumers purchase one service or none. In what follows, we determine the equilibrium under duopoly and monopoly. We restrict our attention to parameter values such that the market is covered in equilibrium.

4.1. Duopoly

417. We start by solving for the equilibrium with single-homing when firm A and B are active.

418. At the fourth stage, a consumer decides on the level of information to the firm she has patronised, let's say firm i. For a given disclosure level d_i and price p_i, the consumer chooses y_i by maximising (1), which gives

$$y_i^c(d_i) = \frac{1}{(1+d_i)^2}. \tag{2}$$

419. From equation (2), we observe that the higher firm i's disclosure level, the less a consumer is willing to provide information, that is, $\partial y_i / \partial d_i \leq 0$.

420. At the third stage, we compute firms' demands by determining the location of the consumer who is indifferent between A and B. Replacing for $y_i^c(d_i)$ into (1), we find that the indifferent consumer is located at

$$x^* = \frac{1}{2} - \frac{p_A - p_B}{2t} + \frac{v}{2t}\left(\frac{1}{1+d_A} - \frac{1}{1+d_B}\right). \tag{3}$$

421. The demand of firm A is therefore $D_A(p_A, p_B) = x^*$, while the demand of firm B is $D_B(p_A, p_B) = 1 - x^*$.

422. At the second stage, firm i sets the selling price of consumer information for the data broker. We assume that firms A and B make a take-it-or-leave-it offer to the data broker, because they represent a bottleneck for access to consumer

107 As in Casadesus-Masanell and Hervas-Drane (2015), firms commit to the level of information disclosure announced in the first stage.

information. The data broker is willing to buy consumer information from i as long as $r_i \leq v^b$. Firm i therefore charges the data broker $r_i = v^b$, and the data broker is left with zero surplus. For simplicity, we normalise v^b to 1, meaning that $r_i = 1$.

423. If the market is covered, firm i's profit is then given by

$$\Pi_i(p_A, p_B) = \left(p_i + d_i y_i^c(d_i)\right) D_i(p_A, p_B). \quad (4)$$

424. From (4), we observe that firm i derives profits from selling its service at a price p_i and from the collection and use of consumer information $d_i y_i^c(d_i)$ at a selling price $r_i = 1$ and a disclosure level d_i.

425. Each firm sets its price p_i to maximise its profit, which is given by given equation (4), taking the rival's price p_j as given. Solving for the price reaction functions, we obtain the equilibrium prices, denoted by $p_i^c\left(d_i, d_j\right)$. Note that as d_i increases, firm i's price decreases, that is, $\partial p_i^c / \partial d_i \leq 0$. The second-order condition is always satisfied, as $\partial^2 \Pi_i / \partial p_i^2 = -1/t < 0$.

426. Plugging equilibrium prices into the profit function (4), we now solve for firms' optimal disclosure levels at Stage 1.

427. Let examine how firm i's profit, which can be written $\Pi_i\left(p_i^c\left(d_i, d_j\right), p_j^c\left(d_i, d_j\right), d_i, d_j\right)$ is affected by a variation of the disclosure level d_i. Using the envelope theorem, we have

$$\frac{d\Pi_i}{dd_i} = \frac{\partial \Pi_i}{\partial d_i} + \frac{\partial \Pi_i}{\partial p_j}\frac{\partial pj^c}{\partial d_i} = \left(d_i \frac{\partial y_i^c}{\partial d_i} + y_i^c\right) D_i + \left(\frac{\partial D_i}{\partial d_i} + \frac{\partial D_i}{\partial p_j}\frac{\partial p_j^c}{\partial d_i}\right)\left(p_i^c + d_i y_i^c\right). \quad (5)$$

428. The first term on the right-hand side of equation (5) represents a direct effect of a higher disclosure level on firm i's revenue from the collecting and using of consumer information. When firm i discloses more information, consumers provide less information ($\partial y_i^c / \partial d_i \leq 0$), which has a negative effect on disclosure revenues. However, this is compensated as firm i collects and uses more consumer information ($y_i^c > 0$). Overall, we find this effect is positive. The second term on the right-hand side of equation of (5) is composed of a direct and an indirect effect. First, a higher disclosure level lowers quality, which induces a negative direct effect on firm i's demand ($\partial D_i / \partial d_i \leq 0$). Second, there is an indirect effect of a higher disclosure level d_i on firm i's demand through firm j's pricing. If consumers have low valuations ($v < (1 - d_i)/(1 + d_i)$), firm j decreases its price when d_i increases, which affects negatively firm i's demand. In contrast, if consumers have high valuations ($v > (1 - d_i)/(1 + d_i)$), firm j reacts to the increase of d_i by increasing its own price p_j, which affects positively firm i's demand. High valuation consumers are more sensitive to quality and perceive more negatively a higher level of disclosure. They have a higher willingness to pay, which induces firm j to increase its price.

429. Each firm sets its disclosure level d_i to maximise its profit, taking the rival's disclosure level d_j as given. Solving for the disclosure reaction functions, we obtain the equilibrium disclosure levels, d_A^c and d_B^c. The second-order conditions are satisfied

at $d_A = d_A^c$ and $d_B = d_B^c$. All consumers are served if the marginal consumer derives a positive utility in equilibrium, that is, if $v / \left(1 + d_i^c\right) - p_i^c - tx^* \geq 0$, i.e. if (i) $0 < v < 1$ and $t \leq (v+1)^2 / 6$, or if (ii) $v \geq 1$ and $t \leq 2v / 3$. We focus on the equilbrium with a covered market and thus that these conditions hold.

430. The following proposition characterises the equilibrium:

431. **Proposition 1.** *In the duopoly equilibrium with a covered market, consumers provide information*

$$y^c = \frac{1}{(1 + d^c)^2}.$$

(i) *If* $0 < v < 1$ *and* $0 < t \leq (v+1)^2 / 6$, *firms' optimal prices and disclosure levels are*

$$p^c = t - \frac{1 - v^2}{4}, \quad d^c = \frac{1 - v}{1 + v}.$$

(ii) *If* $v \geq 1$ *and* $0 < t \leq 2v / 3$, *firms' optimal prices and disclosure levels are*

$$p^c = t, \quad d^c = 0.$$

432. From Proposition 1, we observe that there are two types of equilibria which are represented in Figure 1. If consumers have low valuations ($v < 1$), firms engage in disclosure ($d^c > 0$) and the lower is consumers' willingness to pay for the service, the higher the level of disclosure ($\partial d^c / \partial v \leq 0$), but the lower the provision of information ($\partial y^c / \partial v > 0$). As consumer valuations are low, firms generate lower purchase revenues and disclosure revenues become relatively more important. Firms, which are bottlenecks on consumer information, extract all surplus from the data broker. Firms engaging in disclosure can subsidise consumers by charging negative prices: this happens if consumer valuations are low enough, that is, if $v < 1/5$, or if the level of differentiation is low ($t < \left(1 - v^2 / 4\right)$). Firms subsidise consumers when their valuations are very low while generating more revenues from exploiting their information. Subsidisation also occurs if the level of differentiation is low, that is, if the competitive pressure is strong enough.

433. If consumers willingness to pay for the service is sufficiently high ($v \geq 1$), firms avoid engaging in disclosure ($d^c = 0$), but charge positive prices (higher than if $v < 1$). Indeed, when consumer valuations are high enough, purchase revenues become comparatively more important for firms.

434. In sum, firms face a trade-off between collecting and using consumer information and the level of information provision, which depends on consumer valuations. A higher disclosure level decreases the level of information provision. Consumers with low valuations provide less information, but this information is more exploited to generate larger disclosure revenues. Consumers with high valuations provide more information, but firms generate more value from them through purchase revenues.

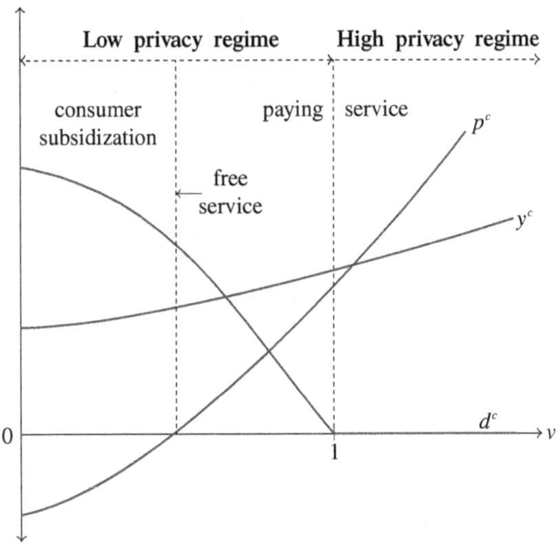

Figure 1 – Equilibrium in single-homing duopoly

4.2. Monopoly

435. We now study the equilibrium when A and B act as a monopoly, for example, after a merger. We consider a multi-product monopoly, which supplies services A and B at prices p_A and p_B, with disclosure levels d_A and d_B, respectively.

436. At Stage 4, the level of information provision y_i for service i is as given in (2): for a given d_i, $y_i^m = 1/(1+d_i)^2$.

437. At Stage 3, if the market is covered, proceeding in a similar way as in the previous sub-section, we find that the demand for service A is $D_A(p_A,p_B) = x^*$ and the demand for service B is $D_B(p_A,p_B) = 1 - x^*$, where x^* is given by (3).

438. In a market which is not covered, we determine the location of the consumer indifferent between buying service i and staying out of the market, that is, $U_i = 0$. The demand for service i in this case is:

$$D_i^u(p_i) = \frac{v}{(1+d_i)t} - \frac{p_i}{t}, \quad i = A,B.$$

439. At Stage 2, we determine the price of consumer information. As in the previous section, the monopolist has monopoly power on consumer information, which is sold at the price $r_A = r_B = 1$.

440. We now consider the pricing problem of the monopoly. If the market is covered, the monopoly profit is given by:

$$\Pi^m(p_A,p_B) = \sum_{i=A,B} \left(p_i + d_i y_i^m(d_i)\right) D_i(p_A,p_B). \tag{6}$$

441. At the optimum for the monopoly with a covered market, the indifferent consumer receives zero surplus, that is, $v / (1 + d_A) - p_A - tx^* = 0$. Substituting for x^* in (3), we obtain the relation between prices that ensures market coverage:

$$p_B = v\left(\frac{1}{1+d_A} + \frac{1}{1+d_B}\right) - p_A - t.$$

442. We can thus express Π^m as a function of only p_A. We solve for the first-order condition $\partial\Pi^m / \partial p_A = 0$ (the second-order condition (SOC) holds as $\partial^2\Pi^m / \partial p_A^2 = -4 / t < 0$), and obtain the equilibrium prices $p_A^m(d_A, d_B)$ and $p_B^m(d_A, d_B)$ when the market is covered.

443. If the market is not covered, the profit of the monopoly is given by

$$\Pi^u(p_A, p_B) = \sum_{i=A,B} \left(p_i + d_i y_i^m(d_i)\right) D_i^u(p_i).$$

444. Profit maximisation yields $p_i^u(d_i) = \left(v(1 + d_i) - d_i\right) / \left(2(1 + d_i)^2\right)$.

445. Consider now the first stage where the monopolist chooses the disclosure levels.

446. If the market is covered, the monopoly sets the disclosure levels to maximise its profit Π^m. Solving for the first-order conditions, we obtain the equilibrium disclosure levels, d_A^m and d_B^m. We check that for these values, the second-order conditions are satisfied.

447. We proceed in a similar way for the uncovered monopoly and obtain $d_i^u = (1 - v) / (1 + v)$.

448. Since we wish to restrict our attention to parameter values such that market is covered, we check under which conditions the monopoly chooses to cover the market. The monopolist covers the market if $\partial\Pi^u / \partial p_i |_{\{p_i = p_i^m, d_i = d_i^m\}} < 0$, which holds if (i) $0 < v < 1$ and $t < (v + 1)^2 / 4$, or if (ii) $v \geq 1$ and $t < v$.

449. The following proposition characterises the monopoly outcome:

450. **Proposition 2.** *In a monopoly with a covered market, consumers provide information*

$$y^m = \frac{1}{(1 + d^m)^2}.$$

(i) If $0 < v < 1$ and $0 < t < (v + 1)^2 / 4$, the monopoly prices and disclosure levels are

$$p^m = \frac{v(1 + v)}{2} - \frac{t}{2}, \quad d^m = \frac{1 - v}{1 + v}.$$

(ii) If $v \geq 1$ and $0 < t < v$, the monopoly prices and disclosure levels are

$$p^m = v - \frac{t}{2}, \quad d^m = 0.$$

451. As in Proposition 1, there are two types of equilibria. The monopolist engages in disclosure ($d^m > 0$) and charges a positive price ($p^m > 0$) if consumer valuations are not too high ($v < 1$). The monopolist charges negative prices if consumer

valuations are very low ($v < 1/3$) and the level of differentiation is high enough ($t > v(1+v)$), while generating larger disclosure revenues. The monopolist charges the maximum price that extracts the surplus of the indifferent consumer. When consumer valuations are low and the differentiation level increases, it is profitable to set negative prices while increasing the level of information disclosure.

452. If consumer valuations are sufficiently high ($v \geq 1$), the monopolist does not engage in disclosure ($d^c = 0$) and charges a positive price. As already explained, the intuition is that when consumer valuations are high, the monopolist relies more on purchase revenues, which are comparatively more beneficial than disclosure revenues.

453. The following proposition compares the duopoly and monopoly outcomes, and examines the impact of competition when consumers single-home.

454. **Proposition 3.** *Moving from duopoly to monopoly*

(i) *is price-increasing ($p_i^d < p_i^m$), but does not eliminate consumers subsidisation (i.e. negative pricing);*

(ii) *has no impact on privacy ($d^c = d^m$).*

455. Proposition 3(i), shows that moving from duopoly to monopoly does not eliminate consumer subsidisation, contrary to Casadesus-Masanell and Hervas-Drane (2015). The particularity of our model is that it incorporates horizontal differentiation. On top of low consumer valuations, a higher level of differentiation (higher t) brings the monopolist to resort to negative pricing. However, a merger to monopoly increases market power: it is price-increasing as it eliminates competition.

456. In Proposition 3(ii), we find that a merger to monopoly does not impact firms' decisions on information disclosure. An explanation is that the firms' incentives to collect and use consumer information are qualitatively the same; there exists a trade-off between exploiting more consumer information (higher disclosure level) and a lower level of information provision from consumers. Moreover, both in monopoly and duopoly, firms are bottlenecks on consumer information.

457. In this framework, a merger to monopoly is profitable in that it increases market power. The merger is privacy-neutral and not data-driven. From the point of view of welfare, it is clear that the merger decreases consumer welfare since for a similar level of information disclosure, consumers, whether they sign up to service A or B, pay a higher price.

5. Multi-Homing

458. We now consider the possibility that some of the consumers purchase both services (i.e. multi-home).

459. **Multi-Homing incentives**. We first characterise how consumers value multi-homing over single-homing. Let $\sigma \in [0,1]$ represent the incremental value of signing up to a second service. If $\sigma = 1$, there is no overlap between the two services and multi-homers derive the full utility from the second service. On the other hand, if $\sigma = 0$, there is a large overlap and the consumption of the second service brings no incremental gross utility.

460. We examine a framework where some consumers choose to single-home, while others choose to multi-home. Figure 2 depicts a possible market outcome, where consumers located to the left of point x_B^0 purchase service A only, those on the right of x_A^0 purchase service B only, and finally consumers between x_B^0 and x_A^0 purchase both.

461. **Utility functions**. The utility of a consumer who purchases service B in addition to service A is

$$U_{A,B} = U_A + \left\{ \sigma v y_B^{1/2} \left(2 - y_B^{1/2} - d_B y_B^{1/2} \right) - p_B - t(1-x) \right\}. \tag{7}$$

462. Similarly, the utility of a consumer who buys service A in addition to service B is

$$U_{B,A} = U_B + \left\{ \sigma v y_A^{1/2} \left(2 - y_A^{1/2} - d_A y_A^{1/2} \right) - p_A - tx \right\}. \tag{8}$$

463. If $\sigma = 0$, the consumer does not benefit from the consumption of a second service.[108] As σ increases, the consumer increasingly values the consumption of a second service, which implies that multi-homing is more valuable. If $\sigma = 1$, there is no overlap between services A and B and $U_{A,B} = U_{B,A}$.

464. **Valuation of multi-homing consumer information**. We finally define how multi-homing consumer information is valued by the data broker. Let αv^b be the value placed by the data broker on the information of each consumer who multi-homes, where $\alpha \in \{0,1\}$. This captures the idea that if multi-homing consumer information is sold twice (i.e. by both firms A and B), it becomes less valuable for the data broker compared to single-homing consumer information, sold only once.[109] We could interpret α as a parameter capturing the attributes of multi-homing consumer information at two extremes: if $\alpha = 0$, multi-homing consumer information is "homogenous", while if $\alpha = 1$, it is "differentiated".[110]

465. In what follows, we firstly examine the duopoly framework. Then, we study a monopolistic market. As in the previous section, we restrict our attention to parameter values such that the market is covered.

466. Note that for the timing at Stage 3, consumers now choose to purchase firm A's or firm B's service, both firms' services, or to stay out of the market.

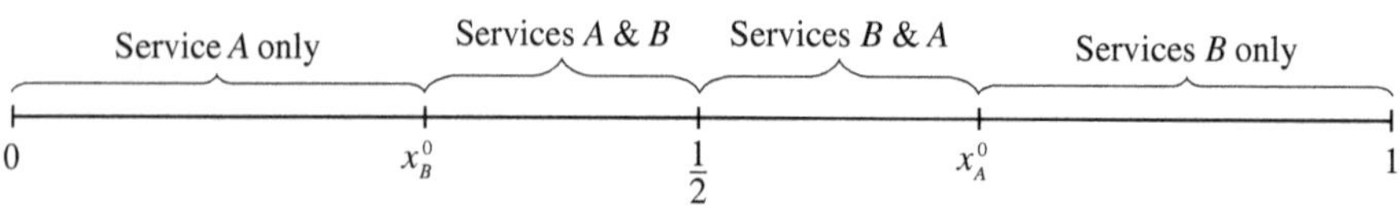

Figure 2 – Demand composition with multi-homing

108 We assume that if $\sigma = 0$, there is no multi-homing, i.e. $p_A + p_B + t > v y_i^{1/2} \left(2 - y_i^{1/2} - d_i y_i^{1/2} \right)$.

109 Anderson, Foros and Kind (2019) use this type of modelling with $\alpha \in [0,1]$. Note that solving our framework with $\alpha \in [0,1]$ generates untractable solutions, which is why we assume $\alpha \in \{0,1\}$.

110 The parameter α is exogenous, meaning that firms do not choose to "make" user information homogenous or differentiated. This stems from the idea that these are the consumers who provide their personal information. We then model two extreme situations where consumers (exogenously) either provide homogenous or differentiated information. For instance, if a consumer provides information on its contacts to firm A while providing information on its photos to firm B, this information is differentiated.

5.1. Duopoly

467. We solve for the equilibrium in the duopoly case.

468. At Stage 4, each consumer decides on the level of information to provide to the firm(s) he has patronised. If the consumer signs up to service i only, he chooses y_i by maximising (1), and the level of information provision is then given by (2). If the consumer signs up to both services, he chooses y_A and y_B to maximise $U_{i,j}$, which gives

$$y_i = \frac{1}{(1+d_i)^2}, \quad i = A,B.$$

469. Therefore, multi-homing and single-homing consumers provide the same level of information when using service i.

470. At Stage 3, consumers choose which service(s) to patronise. With our specification, a consumer who purchases service i in addition to service j does not necessarily derive the same utility as if he purchases j in addition to i, that is, we can have either $U_{AB} > U_{BA}$ or $U_{AB} < U_{BA}$. We therefore make the simplifying assumption that multi-homers to the left of 1/2 sign up to service B in addition to service A and the ones to the right of 1/2 sign up to service A in addition to service B (see Figure 2).[111] We justify this assumption insofar as multi-homers incur disutility from first signing up to a service far from their location; multi-homers to the left of 1/2 (to the right of 1/2) are therefore assumed to primarily sign up to service A (service B). This disutility from location is exogenous to this framework and is simply assumed.

471. The location of the consumer who is indifferent between buying service A and buying both services is then given by $U_A = U_{A,B}$ (location x_B^0 on Figure 2). In a similar way, the location of the consumer who is indifferent as to whether to buy service B and to buy both services is given by $U_B = U_{B,A}$ (location x_A^0 on Figure 2).

472. Let $D_i^s(.)$ be the single-homing demand of firm i and let $D^m(.)$ be the multi-homing demand, common to firms A and B. The single-homing demand of firm i is then

$$D_i^s(p_j) = 1 - \frac{1}{t}\left(\frac{\sigma v}{1+d_j} - p_j\right), \quad i \neq j,$$

473. where $x_B^0 \equiv D_A^s(p_B)$ and $1 - x_A^0 \equiv D_B^s(p_A)$. The multi-homing demand is given by

$$D^m(p_A, p_B) = \frac{\sigma v}{t}\left(\frac{1}{1+d_A} + \frac{1}{1+d_B}\right) - \frac{p_A + p_B}{t} - 1,$$

where $x_A^0 - x_B^0 \equiv D^m(p_A, p_B)$.

---

111 Anderson, Foros, and Kind (2017) specify a utility function where a consumer who purchases service i for its incremental value over service j does so depending on its location x.

474. Firm i's total demand is then given by $D_i = D_i^s + D^m$, that is,

$$D_i(p_i) = \frac{\sigma v}{(1+d_i)t} - \frac{p_i}{t}. \tag{9}$$

475. Firm i's total demand therefore only depends on its own price and disclosure level. However, the composition of firm i's demand in terms of single and multi-homers depends on the prices of the two firms.

476. At Stage 2, firm i determines the selling price of consumer information to the data broker. In our framework, both firms derive revenues from the sale of consumer information. The data broker purchases single-homing user information from firm i if $r_i \leq v^b$. Moreover, the data broker purchases multi-homing user information from both firms is $r_i \leq \alpha v^b$. Assume that firms make a take-it-or-leave-it offer to the data broker. Firm i has a monopoly power over the information of its single-homers, and therefore charges $r_i = v^b = 1$) for access to information about these consumers. By contrast, firms A and B compete for selling information about multi-homers. The equilibrium price depends on the attributes of this information. If $\alpha = 1$, firms provide differentiated information; they are thus bottlenecks and sell multi-homer information at the price $r_A = r_B = 1$. On the other hand, if $\alpha = 0$, firms compete to sell the same information to the data broker; firms lose the advantage of being bottlenecks and in this case, $r_A = r_B = 0$.[112] This implies that multi-homing consumer information is not valuable from the firms.

477. Firm i's profit can then be written as:

$$\Pi_i(p_i) = p_i D_i(p_i) + d_i y_i^c(d_i)\left(D_i^s(p_j) + \alpha D^m(p_i, p_j)\right), \quad \alpha \in \{0,1\}. \tag{10}$$

478. The first part of (10) represents firm i's purchase revenues, while the second part represents the revenues from information disclosure. If $\alpha = 0$, firm i derive revenues from single-homer information only, whereas if $\alpha = 1$, it also generates revenues from the sale of multi-homer information.

479. In what follows, we solve for the equilibrium when $\alpha = 0$, and then when $\alpha = 1$.

Multi-Homing consumer information is homogenous ($\alpha = 0$)

480. Each firm i sets its price p_i to maximise its profit given by (10), taking its rival's price p_j as given. Solving for the first-order conditions of profit maximisation, we obtain the equilibrium price[113]

$$p_i^c(d_i) = \frac{\sigma v}{2(1+d_i)}, \quad i = A, B.$$

481. Plugging the equilibrium prices into the profit function (10), we now solve for the firms' equilibrium disclosure levels at Stage 1.

---

112 Since firms sell "homogenous" information, they compete à la Bertrand, driving prices to zero.

113 The second-order conditions are always satisfied: $\partial^2 \Pi_i / \partial p_i^2 = -2/t < 0$.

482. Let us first examine how firm i's profit $\Pi_i\left(p_i^c(d_i), p_j^c(d_j), d_i, d_j\right)$, is affected by a variation of d_i. With $D_i = D_i^s + D^m$, and using the envelope theorem, we obtain

$$\frac{d\Pi_i}{dd_i} = \left(y_i^c + d_i \frac{\partial y_i^c}{\partial d_i}\right) D_i^s + p_i^c \frac{\partial D_i}{\partial d_i}. \tag{11}$$

483. The first expression in (11) represents a direct (positive) effect of a higher disclosure level on firm i's revenue from exploiting (only) single-homer information. The positive effect of exploiting more consumer information ($y_i^c > 0$) dominates the negative effect that consumers provide less information at the margin ($d_i \partial y_i^c / \partial d_i \le 0$). The second expression in (11) represents a negative direct effect of a higher disclosure level on firm i's total demand. In sum, a higher disclosure level affects positively the revenues from collecting and using single-homing consumer information, but it affects negatively the total demand of the firm (lower quality as disclosure is an inverse measure of quality).

484. Each firm sets its disclosure level d_i to maximise its profit, taking the rival disclosure level d_j as given. Solving for the first-order conditions, we obtain equilibrium disclosure levels, d_A^c and d_B^c. The second-order conditions are satisfied.

485. To ensure that all consumers are served ($U_i \ge 0$ and $U_{i,j} \ge 0$, $i \ne j$) and that there is multi-homing, for all $\sigma \in (0,1]$, the following conditions have to hold:

$$\frac{(\sigma v)^{3/2}}{2} + \frac{\sigma v(1+\sigma v)}{4} < t < \frac{\sigma v(1+\sigma v)}{2} \quad \text{and} \quad 0 < v < \frac{1}{\sigma}, \tag{12a}$$

$$\frac{\sigma v}{2} < t < \sigma v \quad \text{and} \quad v \ge \frac{1}{\sigma}. \tag{12b}$$

486. The following proposition summarises the above results:

487. **Proposition 4** *In the duopoly equilibrium where multi-homing consumer information is homogenous ($\alpha = 0$), the market is covered and consumers provide information*

$$y^c = \frac{1}{(1+d^c)^2}.$$

(i) Given condition (12a), firms' optimal prices and disclosure levels are

$$p\left(d^c\right) = \frac{\sigma v}{2\left(1+d^c\right)}, \quad d^c = \frac{1}{4t}\left(\sigma v(1-\sigma v) + \sqrt{(\sigma v)^2(1-\sigma v)^2 - \sigma v(1+\sigma v)8t + 16t^2}\right).$$

(ii) If $v \ge 1/\sigma$ and $\sigma v / 2 < t < \sigma v$, firms' optimal prices and disclosure levels are

$$p^c = \frac{\sigma v}{2}, \quad d^c = 0.$$

488. There are two types of equilibria for firms competing in prices and information disclosure levels. If consumers have low valuations ($v < 1/\sigma$), firms collect and use consumer information by engaging in disclosure ($d^c > 0$). While a higher disclosure level translates into a lower price ($\partial p^c / \partial d_i < 0$), firms do not subsidise

consumers in exchange for exploiting more consumer information. This result stems from the issue of monetisation of multi-homing consumer information. When maximising its profit, firm i chooses the price that ensures the maximal revenue from the whole demand, that is, from single and multi-homers. Firm i takes into account that it can value the multi-homers only through purchase revenues, which implies that there is no strategic interaction with disclosure revenues. Converserly, firm i can value single-homers through the two revenue channels, which implies a strategic interplay between purchase and disclosure revenues. Since consumer subsidisation may be interesting for single-homers only, firm i does not resort to negative prices.

489. This suggests that as there is more multi-homing, prices should be higher and disclosure levels lower. Let us examine the impact of σ, which is a measure of the incentive to multi-home. We find that as σ increases, firm i increases its price ($\partial p^c / \partial\sigma \geq 0$) and exploits less consumer information ($\partial d^c / \partial\sigma \leq 0$). The intuition is that a higher σ implies that consumer valuation for a second service is higher: a higher valuation implies lower disclosure levels and, in addition, fewer single-homers and therefore fewer possibilities to benefit from exploiting consumer information. The overall effect of a higher σ on firm i's profit is negative ($d\Pi^c / d\sigma \leq 0$). This is explained in particular by the negative impact of σ on firm i's single-homing demand ($dD_i^s / d\sigma < 0$). Note that the data broker benefits from more multi-homing as firms sell (homogenous) multi-homer information at an equilibrium price equal to zero.

490. Finally, as differentiation increases (higher t), firms set a higher disclosure level and a lower price. The intuition is that when there is more differentiation, it is less interesting to multi-home, which implies less multi-homing. As a consequence, there are more single-homers, and firms can better monetise consumer information. Consumer information is more exploited ($\partial d^c / \partial t \geq 0$), which induces firms to decrease prices ($\partial p^c / \partial t \leq 0$).

491. We find different results if consumer valuations are sufficiently high. Indeed, firms do not engage in disclosure ($d^c = 0$) and rely exclusively on purchase revenues. The issue of monetisation of multi-homer information therefore becomes irrelevant. As there is more incentive for multi-homing (higher σ), firms can charge higher prices ($\partial p^c / \partial\sigma \geq 0$). The reason is that as σ is associated to consumer valuation v, firms are able to charge higher prices. The overall effect on profit is positive ($\partial\Pi^c / \partial\sigma \geq 0$).

Multi-Homing consumer information is differentiated ($\alpha = 1$)

492. At Stage 2, each firm sets its price to maximise its profit given (10), taking its rival's price p_j as given. Solving for the first-order conditions of profit maximisation, we obtain the equilibrium price[114]

$$p_i^c(d_i) = \frac{\sigma v(1+d_i) - d_i}{2(1+d_i)^2}, \quad i = A, B.$$

[114] The second-order conditions are always satisfied: where $\partial^2\Pi_i / \partial p_i^2 = -2/t < 0$.

493. A higher disclosure level is associated with a lower price, that is, $\partial p^c / \partial d_i \leq 0$.

494. Plugging the equilibrium prices into the profit function (10), we now solve for firms' optimal disclosure levels at Stage 1.

495. Let us first examine how firm i's profit, $\Pi_i\left(p_i^c(d_i), p_j^c(d_j), d_i, d_j\right)$, is affected by a variation of d_i. Given that $D_i = D_i^s + D^m$, and using the envelope theorem, we obtain

$$\frac{d\Pi_i}{dd_i} = \left(y_i^c + d_i \frac{\partial y_i^c}{\partial d_i}\right) D_i + \left(p_i^c + d_i y_i^c\right) \frac{\partial D_i}{\partial d_i}. \tag{13}$$

496. Compared to equation (11), we observe that in equation (13) the positive effect of a higher disclosure level on firm i's revenue from collecting and using consumer information stems from both single and multi-homing consumers, that is, the total firm's demand. This suggests that firm i should now be able to set a higher disclosure level.

497. Each firm sets its disclosure level d_i to maximise its profit, taking the rival's disclosure level d_j as given. Solving for the first-order conditions, we obtain the equilibrium disclosure levels, d_A^c and d_B^c. The second-order conditions are satisfied.

498. To ensure that all consumers are served (i.e. $U_i \geq 0$ and $U_{i,j} \geq 0$, $i \neq j$) and that there is multi-homing, for all $\sigma \in (0,1]$, the following conditions should hold: (i) $0 < v < 1/\sigma$, $(1+\sigma v)^2/8 < t < (1+\sigma v)^2/4$, or (ii) $v \geq 1/\sigma$ and $\sigma v/2 < t < \sigma v$.

499. The following proposition summarises the analysis:

500. **Proposition 4′.** *In the duopoly equilibrium where multi-homing consumer information is differentiated (* $\alpha = 1$*), the market is covered and consumers provide information*

$$y^c = \frac{1}{(1+d^c)^2}.$$

(i) If $0 < v < 1/\sigma$, $(1+\sigma v)^2/8 < t < (1+\sigma v)^2/4$, *firms' optimal prices and disclosure levels are*

$$p^c = \frac{(1+\sigma v)(3\sigma v - 1)}{8}, \quad d^c = \frac{1-\sigma v}{1+\sigma v}.$$

(ii) If $v \geq 1/\sigma$ *and* $\sigma v/2 < t < \sigma v$, *firms' optimal prices and disclosure levels are*

$$p^c = \frac{\sigma v}{2}, \quad d^c = 0.$$

501. Once again, there are two types of equilibria. If consumer valuations are low ($v < 1/\sigma$), firms engage in disclosure ($d^c > 0$). A lower willingness to pay is associated with a higher disclosure level ($\partial d^c / \partial v \leq 0$) and lower information provision ($\partial y^c / \partial v > 0$). In the meanwhile, when exploiting more consumer information, firms resort to negative pricing if consumer valuations are very low (i.e. $v < 1/3\sigma$). More incentive to multi-home (a higher σ) implies higher prices ($\partial p^c / \partial \sigma > 0$) and lower disclosure levels ($\partial d^c / \partial \sigma \leq 0$). This is because a higher σ implies higher consumer valuations for a

second service and this is negatively associated with the level disclosure. In addition, as σ is higher, firms' profits are also higher ($d\Pi^c / d\sigma \geq 0$). If consumer valuations are sufficiently high, firms charge positive prices and do not engage in disclosure.

502. The following proposition compares firms' decisions depending on the attributes of multi-homer information.

503. **Proposition 5.** *If multi-homing consumer information is homogenous ($\alpha = 0$), firms charge higher prices and set lower disclosure levels compared to the case where consumer information is differentiated ($\alpha = 1$), that is, $p^c_{|\alpha=0} \geq p^c_{|\alpha=1}$ and $d^c_{|\alpha=0} \leq d^c_{|\alpha=1}$, respectively.*

504. The attributes of multi-homing consumer information affect firms' business strategies, in that they modify the trade-off between purchase and disclosure revenues. If $\alpha = 1$, firms represent bottleneck on multi-homing consumer information, contrary to the case where $\alpha = 0$. This implies that firms benefit from setting higher disclosure levels on single-homers only in the latter case, whereas they benefit from it on their whole demand (i.e. including multi-homers) in the former case. Firms therefore sets higher disclosure levels if $\alpha = 1$ compared to $\alpha = 0$. This implies that one should expect different privacy levels depending on how firms monetise multi-homing consumer information.

505. Firms charge higher prices if $\alpha = 0$, as they rely more on purchase revenues. Moreover, they do not make use of negative pricing, contrary to the case where $\alpha = 1$, as they do not sufficiently benefit from exploiting more consumer information in exchange.

506. A higher level of differentiation (a higher t) mitigates the difference between the two cases, $\alpha = 0$ and $\alpha = 1$. Indeed, more differentiation implies less multi-homing, which makes the differences between both cases less pronounced.

5.2. Monopoly

507. In the duopoly, firms cannot derive revenue from multi-homing consumer information if it is homogenous ($\alpha = 0$), as Bertrand competition brings the price of data to zero for these consumers. In this sub-section, we examine if the monopoly is able to internalise this issue.

508. At Stage 4, the level of information y_i is the same as in the previous sub-section: $y_i^c = y_i^m$.

509. At Stage 3, the consumer chooses which service(s) to purchase. Proceeding in a similar way as in the previous sub-section, the demand functions of the monopoly for services A and B are given by equation (9).

510. At Stage 2, the monopolist determines the price of consumer information. We first consider the scenario where multi-homing consumer information is homogenous ($\alpha = 0$), and then the alternative case where it is differentiated ($\alpha = 1$).

Multi-Homing consumer information is homogenous ($\alpha = 0$)

511. The monopolist is a bottleneck on single-homing consumer information and thus charges the data broker $r = 1$. Moreover, the monopolist is now able to monetise

multi-homer information. Indeed, absent any competition, the monopolist sells multi-homer information only once. This creates a bottleneck and multi-homer information is thus sold at $r = 1$.

512. We now characterise the monopoly profit. Let us determine how the revenues from collecting and using multi-homing consumer information appear in the profit function. We assume that a fraction of this information is sold at a disclosure level d_A (i.e. consumers from x_B^0 to 1/2 on the Hotelling line), while the other fraction is sold at a disclosure level d_B (i.e. consumers from 1/2 to x_A^0). This amounts to say that half of all consumer information is sold at a disclosure level d_A, while the other half is sold at a disclosure level d_B.

513. The monopoly profit is thus given by:

$$\Pi^m(p_A ž p_B) = \sum_{i=A,B} p_i D_i(p_i) + \frac{d_i y_i^m(d_i)}{2} \tag{14}$$

514. The monopoly chooses p_A and p_B to maximise (14) by setting $\partial\Pi^m / \partial p_i = 0$. Solving for the first-order conditions, we obtain that $p_i^m = p_i^c$.

515. Plugging the equilibrium prices into the profit function (14), we now solve for the optimal disclosure levels of the monopoly at Stage 1.

516. Let us first examine how the monopoly profit is affected by a variation of the disclosure level d_i. Using the envelope theorem, we obtain

$$\frac{d\Pi^m}{dd_i} = \left(y_i^m + d_i \frac{\partial y_i^m}{\partial d_i} \right) \frac{1}{2} + p_i^c \frac{\partial D_i}{\partial d_i}.$$

517. Compared to equation (11), we observe that disclosure revenues are also generated from multi-homing consumers. Indeed, in the above equation, 1/2 represents the number of single-homers (D_i^s) plus the multi-homers who sign-up to service j in addition to service i (i.e. users from x_A^0 to $1/2$). We therefore have $d\Pi_i^c / dd_i |_{p_i = p_i^c} < d\Pi^m / dd_i |_{p_i = p_i^m}$, which suggests that the equilibrium disclosure level of the monopoly is higher than in duopoly.

518. The monopoly sets its disclosure levels to maximise its profit (14). We obtain the equilibrium disclosure levels d_A^m and d_B^m. The second-order conditions are satisfied.

519. To ensure that all consumers are served (i.e. $U_i \geq 0$ and $U_{i,j} \geq 0$, $i \neq j$) and that there is multi-homing, for $\sigma \in (0,1]$, the following conditions should hold:

$$\frac{\sigma v(1+2\sigma v)}{4} < t < \frac{\sigma v(1+\sigma v)}{2} \quad \text{and} \quad 0 < v \leq \frac{1}{2\sigma}, \tag{15a}$$

$$\sigma^2 v^2 < t < \frac{\sigma v(1+\sigma v)}{2} \quad \text{and} \quad \frac{1}{2\sigma} < v < \frac{1}{\sigma}, \tag{15b}$$

$$\frac{\sigma v}{2} < t < \sigma v \quad \text{and} \quad v \geq \frac{1}{\sigma}. \tag{15c}$$

520. The following proposition summarises the analysis.

521. **Proposition 6.** *In the monopoly equilibrium where multi-homing consumer information is homogenous, consumers provide information*

$$y^m = \frac{1}{(1+d_i^m)^2}.$$

(i) Given conditions (15a-15b), monopoly prices and disclosure levels are

$$p^m = \frac{\sigma v t}{2(2t-(\sigma v)^2)}, \quad d^m = 1 - \frac{(\sigma v)^2}{t}.$$

(ii) If $v \geq 1/\sigma$ and $\sigma v/2 < t < \sigma v$, monopoly prices and disclosure levels are

$$p^m = \frac{\sigma v}{2}, \quad d^m = 0.$$

522. As in Proposition 4, there are two types of equilibria. The monopoly firm engages in disclosure ($d^m > 0$) if consumer valuations are low ($v < 1/\sigma$). The lower consumer valuations are the lower the prices ($\partial p^m / \partial v \geq 0$) but the higher the disclosure levels ($\partial d^m / \partial v \leq 0$). We observe that there is no negative pricing. This stems from the assumption we have made above on how the monopoly exploits multi-homing consumer information (where half of consumer information is sold at disclosure level d_A while the other half is sold at disclosure level d_B).[115]

523. As there is more incentive to multi-home (higher σ), the monopoly increases prices ($\partial p^m / \partial \sigma \geq 0$), but sets lower disclosure levels ($\partial d^m / \partial \sigma \leq 0$). As already explained, a higher σ is associated with higher consumer valuations, which induces the firm to lower the level of disclosure. The effect of a higher σ on profit is positive ($\partial \Pi^m / \partial \sigma \geq 0$). This is because the issue of monetisation of multi-homer information has been internalised by the monopoly; a higher σ has therefore a positive effect on the firm's profit, unlike in the duopoly.

524. A higher level of differentiation (t) induces the monopoly to increase disclosure levels and to decrease prices. This is due to the fact that as t increases, there are fewer multi-homers, which implies that the firm is better able to collect and use consumer information.

525. If consumer valuations are sufficiently high ($v \geq 1/\sigma$), the monopoly does not engage in disclosure ($d^m = 0$) and relies only on purchase revenues only ($p^m > 0$). More incentive to multi-home translates into higher prices and a higher profit.

526. We now compare the monopoly and the duopoly outcomes with the following proposition:

527. **Proposition 7.** *If multi-homing consumer information is homogenous ($\alpha = 0$), a merger to monopoly is data-driven and harms consumers.*

---

115 Another way to model the monopoly would be to assume that all multi-homing consumer information is sold at a disclosure level d_i so that consumer information for users located between 0 and x_A^0 are disclosed at a level d_A, while users located between x_A^0 and 1 are disclosed at a level d_B. A first issue is that it gives complex formulas (in particular for d_B), which are barely tractable. A second issue is to check whether an equilibrium exists when $d_A = d_B$, while the incentives for the monopoly to charge d_A and d_B are not the same.

528. Moving from duopoly to monopoly mitigates the issue of the monetisation of multi-homer information, since the monopoly firm internalises this issue. In this respect, a merger to monopoly is data-driven. The monopolist is able to monetise multi-homing consumer information so that it can better rely on disclosure revenues. In this way, it increases the level of disclosure ($d^c \leq d^m$) and strategically lowers the price ($p^c \geq p^m$).

529. A merger to monopoly therefore decreases prices and privacy levels. It harms consumer welfare ($CS^d > CS^m$), while it increases produces surplus ($\Pi^m > 2\Pi^c$). The effect on total welfare depends on the values of the parameters; the merger can be either welfare-decreasing or increasing.

530. Note that the differences in price and disclosure are less significant as the level of differentiation increases. Indeed, we have $\partial d^c / \partial t > \partial d^m / \partial t$ and $\left|\partial p^c / \partial t\right| > \left|\partial p^m / \partial t\right|$.

Multi-Homing consumer information is differentiated ($\alpha = 1$)

531. We solve this case in similar way as in the duopoly; the only change is that there is joint profit maximisation for services *A* and *B*. Given that demands for services *A* and *B* are independent in that they only depend on their own price and disclosure level (i.e. $D_i = D_i(p_i, d_i)$), we obtain the same results for prices and disclosure levels, as in duopoly (Proposition 4').

532. We therefore state the following proposition.

533. **Proposition 8** *If multi-homing consumer information is differentiated ($\alpha = 1$), a merger to monopoly is welfare-neutral.*

534. Moving from duopoly to monopoly modifies neither prices nor disclosure levels. In the Hotelling specification of multi-homing,a firm's total demand is independent of price and disclosure level of the rival, which implies that duopoly firms have monopoly power on their total demand.[116] The monopoly, which is multi-product, does not change this situation. In addition, the incentives to set a given disclosure level are similar. Duopoly firms are bottlenecks on consumer information, and a merger to monopoly does not modify this. For these reasons, a merger to monopoly has no effect and is welfare-neutral. Apart from monopolising the market, firms have no incentive to merge.

6. Conclusion

535. In this chapter, we examine the impact of competition between firms in prices and information disclosure levels.

536. We find that firms adopt two types of business strategies characterised by a trade-off between the collection and use of consumer information, the level of information

116 However, there is still strategic interaction between single and multi-homing demands. For instance, if the rival firm (say, firm *B*) increases its price or its disclosure level, this increases (decreases) the single-homing (multi-homing) demand of firm *A*; in other words, this affects firm *A*'s demand composition.

provision, and consumer valuations. When consumers have low valuations, we show that firms engage in the disclosure of consumer information (low-privacy regime): the lower consumer valuations are, the more firms exploit consumer information, but the lower the level of information provision. Firms can even resort to negative pricing if their valuations are very low or if the competition intensity in the market is high enough. Firms, which are bottlenecks on consumer information, charge the data broker the monopoly price, leaving her with zero surplus. Second, if consumers have high valuations, we show that firms do not engage in disclosure of consumer information (high-privacy regime) and charge positive prices.

537. If consumers single-home, we find that a merger to monopoly increases market power but is privacy-neutral. However, when we consider multi-homing, we find that firms' business strategies are altered and depend on multi-homing incentives, competition intensity, and their ability to monetise multi-homer information. In particular, if multi-homer information is homogenous (i.e. firms compete for selling the same information to the data broker), firms are unable to generate disclosure revenues from multi-homers. We show that in this case, a merger to monopoly improves the firms' ability to monetise multi-homer information. The merger decreases prices and privacy levels, and harms consumers.

538. The possibility of consumer multi-homing introduces more complexity to firms' business models. Indeed, firms choose the level of privacy of their service not only by taking into account consumer valuations as in the single-homing benchmark, but also by considering the incentives to multi-home, competition intensity (product differentiation) and the monetisation of multi-homer information. Our results suggest that in presence of a merger to monopoly, great attention should be paid to the importance of consumer multi-homing. Indeed, if the merger is data-driven (e.g. to better motenise multi-homer data), it may harm consumers by decreasing privacy, that is, service quality.

539. In this analysis, we study the link between privacy, competition, and consumer purchase behaviour, that is, single and multi-homing. However, our analysis relies on a reduced-form model, with a specific utility function. A direction for further research would therefore be to generalise the model, for instance by generalising the utility function. Moreover, it would be interesting to examine our framework by allowing the attributes of multi-homer information (α) to vary between 0 and 1 in order to give more intuitions about the impact of multi-homing on firms' business strategies.

Appendix

Framework of Casadesus-Masanell and Hervas-Drane (2015)

540. We solve their model in a horisontal differentiation framework.

541. The net utility of the consumer, located at $x \in [0,1]$, when purchasing service i, for given price p_i and information disclosure $d_i \in [0,1]$, is

$$U_i = vy_i(1 - y_i - d_i) - p_i - tx,$$

where $v > 0$ is the intrinsic benefit of the service, and transportation costs are equal to tx for firm A and to $t(1 - x)$ for firm B.

Duopoly

542. **Stage 4.** A consumer chooses the level of information provision to the firm she has patronised, say firm i, by maximising U_i with respect to y_i, which gives

$$y_i^c = \frac{1 - d_i}{2}.$$

543. **Stage 3.** The consumer who is indifferent between purchasing service A and service B is given by

$$x^* = \frac{1}{2} - \frac{p_A - p_B}{2t} + \frac{v}{8t}\left((1 - d_A)^2 - (1 - d_B)^2\right),$$

where $D_A(p_A, p_B) = x^*$ and $D_B(p_A, p_B) = 1 - x^*$.

544. **Stage 2.** The selling price of consumer information is the monopoly price, that is, $p_i^b = 1$. Firm i chooses the price p_i that maximises its profit, given the rival's price p_j. It then solves

$$\max_{p_i} \Pi_i(p_A, p_B), \quad \text{where} \quad \Pi_i(p_A, p_B) = \left(p_i + d_i y_i^c(d_i)\right) D_i(p_A, p_B).$$

545. Firm i's equilibrium price is $p_i^c(d_A, d_B)$ (the SOCs are satisfied: $\partial^2 \Pi_i / \partial p_i^2 = -1 / t < 0$).

546. **Stage 1.** Firm i chooses the disclosure level d_i that maximises its profit, given the rival's disclosure level d_j. Plugging the equilibrium prices $p_A^c(d_A, d_B)$ and $p_B^c(d_A, d_B)$ into the profit function, firm i maximises $\Pi_i(d_A, d_B)$ with respect to d_i. We find that the equilibrium disclosure level (such that the second order conditions are satisfied) are symmetric and given by $d_i^c = (1 - v) / (2 - v)$.

547. To ensure that all consumers are served, that is, $U_i \geq 0$, the following conditions should hold: (i) $0 < v < 1$ and $0 < t \leq 1/6(2-v)$ or (ii) $v \geq 1$ and $0 < t \leq v/6$.

548. **Result 1.** *In the duopoly equilibrium, the market is covered and consumers provide information*

$$y^c = \frac{1}{(1+d^c)^2}.$$

(i) If $0 < v < 1$ *and* $0 < t \leq 1/6(2-v)$*, firms' optimal prices and disclosure levels are*

$$p^c = \frac{v-1}{2(v-2)^2} + t, \quad d^c = \frac{1-v}{2-v}.$$

(ii) If $v \geq 1$ *and* $0 < t \leq v/6$*, firms' optimal prices and disclosure levels are*

$$p^c = t, \quad d^c = 0.$$

Monopoly

549. **Stage 4.** We obtain the same information provision function at Stage 4, as in the duopoly.

550. **Stage 3.** If the monopolist covers the market, the indifferent consumer is defined in the same way as in the duopoly. If the monopoly does not cover the market, the monopoly demand for service i is (i.e. the consumer who is indifferent between purchasing service i and staying out of the market)

$$D_i^u(p_i) = \frac{v(1-d_i)^2}{4t} - \frac{p_i}{t}.$$

551. **Stage 2.** From the profit maximisation of the covered monopoly, we get $p_i^m(d_A, d_B)$. For the uncovered monopoly, we obtain

$$p_i^u(d_i) = \frac{(1-d_i)(v(1-d_i)-2d_i)}{8}.$$

552. **Stage 1.** Solving for the equilibrium disclosure levels of the covered and uncovered monopolies, we find that $d_i^m = d_i^u = (1-v)/(2-v)$.

553. To determine the range of values for which the monopolist covers the market, we solve $\partial\Pi^u / \partial p_i |_{\{p_i = p_i^m, d_i = d_i^m\}} < 0$. The monopolist covers the market if (i) $0 < v < 1$ and $t < 1/4(2-v)$, or if (ii) $v \geq 1$ and $t < v$.

554. **Result 2.** *The monopolist chooses to cover the market in equilibrium and consumers buying service i provide information*

$$y^m = \frac{1}{(1+d^m)^2}$$

(*i*) *If* $0 < v < 1$ *and* $0 < t < 1/4(2 - v)$, *the monopoly prices and disclosure levels for services A and B are*

$$p^m = \frac{v}{4(2-v)^2} - \frac{t}{2}, \quad d^m = \frac{1-v}{2-v}.$$

(*ii*) *If* $v \geq 1$ *and* $0 < t < v$, *the monopoly prices and disclosure levels for services A and B are*

$$p^m = v - \frac{t}{2}, \quad d^m = 0.$$

GENERAL CONCLUSION

555. This books aims to contribute to the analysis of firms' strategies in network industries, which are a critical driver of economic growth and characterised by a fast pace of evolution. What follows briefy summarises the main results of the three chapters and suggests general directions for further research.

556. In the first chapter of the thesis, I examine firms' incentives to merge in-market vs cross-border and the impact of merger policy.

557. I find that in a scenario where an exit-by-merger is impossible, a stricter (more lenient) merger policy shifts firms' decisions towards cross-border mergers (in-market mergers). However, if it is possible to exit by merger, I show that the merger policy also affects the incentives to merge cross-border, thereby modifying the trade-off between merger types. The underlying idea of this analysis is that if the merger policy were very strict and market-level synergies were low (i.e. the payoff from merging would be low), firms would ultimately not merge at all. From a policy point of view, the results suggest that the merger policy should consider subsequent mergers triggered by an initial decision to merge, which here corresponds to the scenario of an exit-by-merger after a failed cross-border merger. The results also suggest that, in general, the ease of entry into a market (such as entry in a foreign market through a cross-border merger) can be affected by the severity of merger policy, the reason being that it may increase the barriers to exit.

558. In the second chapter of the thesis, we investigate the impact of competition between a private firm and public firms on prices and investment in new infrastructures. We consider two scenarios of public intervention: with a national public firm and with local public firms.

559. In a monopoly benchmark, we show that the private firm charges the monopoly price and covers up to an area where the monopoly profit is equal to the marginal cost of investment. The national public firm, which never charges more than the monopoly price, sets a price such that it cross-subsidises between low-cost and high-cost areas, which allows it to cover a larger share of the country than the private firm. Local public firms, which charge prices contingent on the investment cost in their own area, charge no more than the monopoly price and cover the same areas as the private firm.

560. When the national public firm has invested more than the private firm, we find that prices are strategic complements for the private firm and are strategic substitutes for the national public firm. A larger overlap between the private firm's and the public firm's networks drives firms' prices up. In the equilibrium of the coverage-price game, total coverage by the national public firm is lower than in the benchmark. Competition leads the private firm to set lower prices than in the benchmark, while the public firm may charge higher prices than in the benchmark; this can be explained by the competition from the private firm, which makes it harder to sustain low prices.

561. When the local public firms have invested more than the private firm, we find that a larger overlap between the private firm's network and the local public firms' networks leads to a higher price by the private firm and lower prices by the local public firms. In the equilibrium of the coverage-price game, total coverage is the same than in the benchmark. The private firm sets a lower price as in the benchmark, while the local public firms set higher prices.

562. The results suggest that in grey areas, public investment in a network infrastructure may not always be the most suitable method of public intervention. It depends on the market conditions, which means that a policymaker has to make a complex trade-off between the nature of competition, its intensity, and the costs of network duplication. This also involves the consideration of the opportunity cost of financial public intervention (public investment) compared to regulation.

563. The third chapter examines the impact of competition between firms in prices and information disclosure levels.

564. We show that firms adopt two types of business strategies, characterised by a trade-off between the collection and use of consumer information, the level of information provision, and consumer valuations. If consumer valuations are sufficiently low, firms engage in the disclosure of consumer information (low-privacy regime): the lower consumer valuations are, the more firms exploit consumer information, but the lower the level of information provision. Firms even set negative prices for consumers if their valuations are very low or if competition intensity is high in the market. Firms represent bottlenecks on consumer information, and leave the data broker with zero surplus. On the other hand, if consumer valuations are sufficiently high, firms do not engage in disclosure of consumer information (high-privacy regime) and always charge positive prices.

565. If consumers can only single-home, a merger to monopoly increases market power but is privacy-neutral. When we consider the possibility of multi-homing, we show that firms' business strategies are altered and depend on multi-homing incentives, competition intensity, and on firms' ability to monetise multi-homer information. More precisely, if firms are unable to generate revenues from the information provided by multi-homers, firms charge higher prices and set lower disclosure levels compared to the case where they can monetise this information. The surplus of the data broker increases as there are more multi-homers. We find that a merger to monopoly improves the firms' ability to monetise multi-homer information. The merger decreases prices and privacy levels, and harms consumers.

566. The results suggest that in presence of a merger to monopoly, great attention should be paid to the importance of consumer multi-homing. Indeed, if the merger is data-driven (e.g. to better motenise multi-homer data), it may harm consumers by decreasing privacy, that is, service quality.

567. Over recent decades, network industries have constantly and rapidly evolved. This evolution has been possible thanks to adapted regulatory and competition policy frameworks. A crucial determinant of future evolutions in network industries is digital transformation. This is a hot topic for public authorities as new digital technologies (e.g. the fifth generation mobile network, 5G) are expected to profoundly modify market structures and firms' business strategies. One can expect that regulators and competition authorities will face new challenges.

568. Further research is needed to understand the functioning of new markets arising subsequently to the introduction of a new digital technology, such as 5G. Questions may arise around the necessity of public intervention but also about the impact of firms' strategies on consumer welfare. In this respect, one can reasonably think that the research questions examined in this book will remain relevant.

BIBLIOGRAPHY

Acquisti, Alessandro, Curtis Taylor, and Liad Wagman (2016) "The economics of privacy," *Journal of Economic Literature*, Vol. 54, pp. 442–92.

Anderson, Simon P, Oystein Foros, and Hans Jarle Kind (2017) "Product functionality, competition, and multipurchasing," *International Economic Review*, Vol. 58, pp. 183–210.

——(2019) "The importance of consumer multihoming (joint purchases) for market performance: Mergers and entry in media markets," *Journal of Economics & Management Strategy*, Vol. 28, pp. 125–137.

Anderson, Simon P and Joshua S Gans (2011) "Platform siphoning: Ad-avoidance and media content," *American Economic Journal: Microeconomics*, Vol. 3, pp. 1–34.

Anton, James J, James H Vander Weide, and Nikolaos Vettas (2002) "Entry auctions and strategic behavior under cross-market price constraints," *International Journal of Industrial Organization*, Vol. 20, pp. 611–629.

ARCEP (2007) "Rapport public d'activité," URL: http://www.arcep.fr/uploads/tx_gspublication/rap2006-light.zip.

Armstrong, Mark (2006) "Competition in two-sided markets," *The RAND Journal of Economics*, Vol. 37, pp. 668–691.

Armstrong, Mark and Helen Weeds (2007) "Programme quality in subscription and advertising-funded television," *Unpublished working paper*.

Autorite de la Concurrence and Bundeskartellamt (2016) "Data and Competition Law," URL: https://www.autoritedelaconcurrence.fr/sites/default/files/rapport-concurrence-donnees-vf-mai2016.pdf.

Bacache, Maya, Marc Bourreau, and Germain Gaudin (2014) "Dynamic entry and investment in new infrastructures: Empirical evidence from the fixed broadband industry," *Review of Industrial Organization*, Vol. 44, pp. 179–209.

Baranes, Edmond and Andreea Cosnita-Langlais (2016) "Les defis poses par l'economie numerique aux politiques de concurrence," in *Annales des Mines-Realites industrielles*, No. 3, pp. 28–31, FFE.

Baumol, Panzar and John Panzar (1982) "Contestable Markets and the Theory of Industry Structure," *New York*.

Beato, P and A Mas-Colell (1984) "The marginal cost pricing as a regulation mechanism in mixed markets": in Marchand, M, Pestieau, P., and H. Tulkens, eds., The Performance of Public Enterprises."

Bech-Bruun, European Commission, and Lexidale (2016) "Study on the application of the Cross-Border Mergers Directive," URL: https://publications.europa.eu/en/publication-detail/-/publication/0291c60a-df7a-11e5-8fea-01aa75ed71a1.

Belleflamme, Paul and Martin Peitz (2019) "Platform competition: Who benefits from multihoming?" *International Journal of Industrial Organization*, Vol. 64, pp. 1–26.

Bjorvatn, Kjetil (2004) "Economic integration and the profitability of cross-border mergers and acquisitions," *European Economic Review*, Vol. 48, pp. 1211–1226.

Bourreau, Marc (2016) *Regulation des communications electroniques*: Lavoisier Paris.

Bourreau, Marc, Carlo Cambini, and Pinar Dogan (2012) "Access pricing, competition, and incentives to migrate from "old" to "new" technology," *International Journal of Industrial Organization*, Vol. 30, pp. 713–723.

——(2014) "Access regulation and the transition from copper to fiber networks in telecoms," *Journal of Regulatory Economics*, Vol. 45, pp. 233–258.

Bourreau, Marc, Carlo Cambini, and Steffen Hoernig (2015) "Geographic access markets and investments," *Information Economics and Policy*, Vol. 31, pp. 13–21.

——(2018) "Cooperative investment, access, and uncertainty," *International Journal of Industrial Organization*, Vol. 56, pp. 78–106.

Bourreau, Marc and Pinar Doğan (2006) "Build or buy strategies in the local loop," *American Economic Review*, Vol. 96, pp. 72–76.

Bourreau, Marc, Richard Feasey, and Ambre Nicolle (2020) "Assessing fifteen years of State Aid for broadband in the European Union: A quantitative analysis," *Telecommunications Policy*, Vol. 44, p. 101974.

Bourreau, Marc, Johan Hombert, Jerome Pouyet, and Nicolas Schutz (2011) "Upstream competition between vertically integrated firms," *The Journal of Industrial Economics*, Vol. 59, pp. 677–713.

Bourreau, Marc and Bruno Jullien (2018) "Mergers, investments and demand expansion," *Economics Letters*, Vol. 167, pp. 136–141.

Breinlich, Holger, Volker Nocke, and Nicolas Schutz (2016) "International aspects of merger policy: a survey," *International Journal of Industrial Organization*, Vol. 50, pp. 415–429.

Briglauer, Wolfgang, Christian Holzleitner, and Ingo Vogelsang (2016) "The need for more efficient public funding of new communications infrastructure in EU member states," *Information Economics and Policy*, Vol. 36, pp. 26–35.

Brito, Duarte (2005) "Should alternative mergers or acquisitions be considered by antitrust authorities?" *International Journal of Industrial Organization*, Vol. 23, pp. 129–153.

Brito, Duarte and Pedro Pereira (2010) "Access to bottleneck inputs under oligopoly: a prisoners' dilemma?" *Southern Economic Journal*, Vol. 76, pp. 660–677.

Brynjolfsson, Erik, Lorin M Hitt, and Heekyung Hellen Kim (2011) "Strength in numbers: How does data-driven decisionmaking affect firm performance?" *Available at SSRN 1819486.*

Bundeskartellamt (2016) "The Market Power of Platforms and Networks, Executive Summary," *Working Paper.*

Caillaud, Bernard and Bruno Jullien (2003) "Chicken & egg: Competition among intermediation service providers," *RAND journal of Economics*, Vol. 34, pp. 309–328.

Calzolari, Giacomo and Alessandro Pavan (2006) "On the optimality of privacy in sequential contracting," *Journal of Economic theory*, Vol. 130, pp. 168–204.

Casadesus-Masanell, Ramon and Andres Hervas-Drane (2015) "Competing with privacy," *Management Science*, Vol. 61, pp. 229–246.

Cave, Martin (2006) "Encouraging infrastructure competition via the ladder of investment," *Telecommunications Policy*, Vol. 30, pp. 223–237.

Cave, Martin and Ian Martin (2010) "Motives and means for public investment in nationwide next generation networks," *Telecommunications Policy*, Vol. 34, pp. 505–512.

CERRE (2015) "Affordability of utilities' services: extent, practice, policy," URL: https://www.cerre.eu/sites/cerre/files/Affordability_ResearchPaper_3.pdf.

——(2020a) "BigTech acquisitions: competition and innovation effects & EU merger control," URL: https://cerre.eu/wp-content/uploads/2020/03/cerre_big_tech_acquisitions_merger_control_EU_2020.pdf.

——(2020b) "Cooperation between firms to deploy very high capacity networks," URL: https://cerre.eu/wp-content/uploads/2020/11/REPORT_Cooperation-between-firms-to-deploy-very-high-capacity-networks_CERRE_November2020.pdf.

Chaudhuri, Amrita (2014) "Cross-Border Mergers and Market Segmentation," *The Journal of Industrial Economics*, Vol. 62, pp. 229–257.

Choi, Jay Pil (2010) "Tying in two-sided markets with multi-homing," *The Journal of Industrial Economics*, Vol. 58, pp. 607–626.

Choi, Jay Pil, Doh-Shin Jeon, and Byung-Cheol Kim (2019) "Privacy and personal data collection with information externalities," *Journal of Public Economics*, Vol. 173, pp. 113–124.

Chone, Philippe, Laurent Flochel, and Anne Perrot (2000) "Universal service obligations and competition," *Information Economics and Policy*, Vol. 12, pp. 249–259.

——(2002) "Allocating and funding universal service obligations in a competitive market," *International Journal of Industrial Organization*, Vol. 20, pp. 1247–1276.

Chone, Philippe and Laurent Linnemer (2008) "Assessing horizontal mergers under uncertain efficiency gains," *International Journal of Industrial Organization*, Vol. 26, pp. 913–929.

Crawford Gregory, Caffara Cristina, Valletti Tommaso (2020) "How tech rolls: Potential competition and reverse killer acquisitions," URL: https://voxeu.org/content/how-tech-rolls-potential-competition-and-reverse-killer-acquisitions.

Cremer, Helmuth, Maurice Marchand, and Jacques-Francois Thisse (1989) "The public firm as an instrument for regulating an oligopolistic market," *Oxford Economic Papers*, pp. 283–301.

Cremer, Jacques, Montjoye Yves Alexandre, and Schweitzer Heike (2019) "Competition policy for the digital era," URL: https://ec.europa.eu/research/industrial_technologies/pdf/factsheet-cppp_en.pdf, European Commission report.

De Corniere, Alexandre and Romain De Nijs (2016) "Online advertising and privacy," *The RAND Journal of Economics*, Vol. 47, pp. 48–72.

De Fraja, Giovanni and Flavio Delbono (1989) "Alternative strategies of a public enterprise in oligopoly," *Oxford Economic Papers*, Vol. 41, pp. 302–311.

Dertwinkel-Kalt, Markus and Christian Wey (2016) "Structural remedies as a signaling device," *Information Economics and Policy*, Vol. 35, pp. 1–6.

Dosis, Anastasios and Wilfried Sand-Zantman (2021) "The ownership of data," *Working Paper*.

Duch-Brown, Nestor, Marten Bertin, and Mueller-Langer Frank (2017) "The economics of ownership, access and trade in digital data," URL: https://ec.europa.eu/jrc/sites/jrcsh/files/jrc104756.pdf, JRC Digital Economy Working Paper 2017-01.

European Commission (2004) "EU Merger Regulation," URL: https://eur-lex.europa.eu/legal-content/EN/TXT/PDF/?uri=CELEX:32004R0139 from=EN.

——(2006) "Study of the performance of network industries providing services of general economic interest," URL: http://ec.europa.eu/economy_finance/publications/pages/publication9603_en.pdf.

——(2009) "Community guidelines for the application of state aid rules in relation to rapid deployment of broadband networks," URL: https://eur-lex.europa.eu/legal-content/EN/TXT/PDF/?uri=CELEX:52009XC0930(02) from=EN.

——(2010) "Commission recommendation of 20 September 2010 on regulated access to Next Generation Access Networks (NGA)," URL: https://eur-lex.europa.eu/legal-content/EN/TXT/PDF/?uri=CELEX:32010H0572 from=FR.

——(2011) "State aid in the form of public service compensation," URL: http://ec.europa.eu/smart-regulation/impact/ia_carried_out/docs/ia_2011/sec_2011_1581_en.pdf.

——(2013) "EU guidelines for the application of the State Aid rule," URL: https://eur-lex.europa.eu/LexUriServ/LexUriServ.do?uri=OJ:C:2013:025:0001:0026:EN:PDF.

——(2014) "White Paper: Towards more effective EU merger control," URL: https://eur-lex.europa.eu/legal-content/EN/TXT/PDF/?uri=CELEX:52014DC0449 from=EN.

——(2017a) "Enter the Data Economy," URL: https://ec.europa.eu/epsc/sites/epsc/files/strategic_note_issue_21.pdf, EPSC Strategic Notes.

——(2017b) "EU merger control: how to remove anti-competitive effects?," URL: http://ec.europa.eu/competition/speeches/text/sp2017_23_en.pdf.

European Parliament (2016) "Broadband as a universal service," URL: http://www.europarl.europa.eu/RegData/etudes/BRIE/2016/581977/EPRS_BRI(2016)581977_EN.pdf, European Parliamentary Research Service.

Farrell, Joseph and Carl Shapiro (1990) "Horizontal mergers: an equilibrium analysis," *The American Economic Review*, pp. 107–126.

Federal Trade Commission and US Department of Justice (2010) "Horizontal merger guidelines," URL: https://www.ftc.gov/sites/default/files/attachments/merger-review/100819hmg.pdf.

Foros, 0ystein (2004) "Strategic investments with spillovers, vertical integration and foreclosure in the broadband access market," *International journal of industrial organization*, Vol. 22, pp. 1–24.

Foros, Oystein and Hans Jarle Kind (2003) "The broadband access market: Competition, uniform pricing and geographical coverage," *Journal of Regulatory Economics*, Vol. 23, pp. 215–235.

Gautier, Axel and Xavier Wauthy (2010) "Price competition under universal service obligations," *International Journal of Economic Theory*, Vol. 6, pp. 311–326.

Genakos, Christos, Tommaso Valletti, and Frank Verboven (2018) "Evaluating market consolidation in mobile communications," *Economic Policy*, Vol. 33, pp. 45–100.

Haufler, Andreas and Soren Bo Nielsen (2007) "Merger policy to promote global players? A simple model," *Oxford Economic Papers*, Vol. 60, pp. 517–545.

Hauge, Janice A, Mark A Jamison, and Richard J Gentry (2008) "Bureaucrats as entrepreneurs: Do municipal telecommunications providers hinder private entrepreneurs?" *Information Economics and Policy*, Vol. 20, pp. 89–102.

Hermalin, Benjamin E and Michael L Katz (2006) "Privacy, property rights and efficiency: The economics of privacy as secrecy," *Quantitative Marketing and Economics*, Vol. 4, pp. 209–239.

Hoernig, Steffen H (2006) "Should uniform pricing constraints be imposed on entrants?" *Journal of Regulatory Economics*, Vol. 30, pp. 199–216.

Horn, Henrik and Lars Persson (2001) "The equilibrium ownership of an international oligopoly," *Journal of International Economics*, Vol. 53, pp. 307–333.

Hui, Kai-Lung and PL Ivan (2006) "Png. 2006," *The Economics of Privacy*, pp. 471–498.

Jaunaux, Laure, Yassine Lefouili, and Wilfried Sand-Zantman (2017) "Entry and merger policy," *Economics Letters*, Vol. 161, pp. 124–129.

Jeanjean, François and Georges Vivien Houngbonon (2017) "Market structure and investment in the mobile industry," *Information Economics and Policy*, Vol. 38, pp. 12–22.

Jullien, Bruno, Jerome Pouyet, and Wilfried Sand-Zantman (2010) "Public and private investments in regulated network industries: coordination and competition issues," *Review of Network Economics*, Vol. 9.

——(2017) "An offer you can't refuse: early contracting with endogenous threat," *The RAND Journal of Economics*, Vol. 48, pp. 733–748.

——(2018) "Quel role pour les acteurs publics dans l'incitation privee aux investissements?" *Revue Économique*, Vol. 69, pp. 985–1007.

Lee, Sang-Ho, Toshihiro Matsumura, and Susumu Sato (2018) "An analysis of entry-then-privatization model: welfare and policy implications," *Journal of Economics*, Vol. 123, pp. 71–88.

Lefouili, Yassine and Ying Lei Toh (2018) "Privacy and quality," *TSE Working Paper 17 (795)*.

Lommerud, Kjell Erik, Odd Rune Straume, and Lars Sorgard (2006) "National versus international mergers in unionized oligopoly," *The RAND Journal of Economics*, Vol. 37, pp. 212–233.

Marino, Anthony M and Jan Zabojnik (2006) "Merger, ease of entry and entry deterrence in a dynamic model," *The Journal of Industrial Economics*, Vol. 54, pp. 397–423.

Mason, Robin and Helen Weeds (2013) "Merger policy, entry, and entrepreneurship," *European Economic Review*, Vol. 57, pp. 23–38.

Matsumura, Toshihiro (1998) "Partial privatization in mixed duopoly," *Journal of Public Economics*, Vol. 70, pp. 473–483.

McAfee, R Preston and Michael A Williams (1992) "Horizontal mergers and antitrust policy," *The Journal of Industrial Economics*, pp. 181–187.

Merrill, William C and Norman Schneider (1966) "Government firms in oligopoly industries: a short-run analysis," *The Quarterly Journal of Economics*, Vol. 80, pp. 400–412.

Montes, Rodrigo, Wilfried Sand-Zantman, and Tommaso Valletti (2018) "The value of personal information in online markets with endogenous privacy," *Management Science*, Vol. 65, pp. 1342–1362.

Motta, Massimo and Emanuele Tarantino (2021) "The effect of horizontal mergers, when firms compete in prices and investments," *International Journal of Industrial Organization, Forthcoming)*.

Motta, Massimo and Helder Vasconcelos (2005) "Efficiency gains and myopic antitrust authority in a dynamic merger game," *International Journal of Industrial Organization*, Vol. 23, pp. 777–801.

Nitsche, Rainer and Lars Wiethaus (2011) "Access regulation and investment in next generation networks: A ranking of regulatory regimes," *International Journal of Industrial Organization*, Vol. 29, pp. 263–272.

Noam, Eli (1995a) "Privacy in telecommunications, part I," *New Telecommunications Quarterly*, Vol. 3, pp. 51–59.

——(1995b) "Privacy in telecommunications, part III," *New Telecommunications Quarterly*, Vol. 3, pp. 52–69.

Nocke, Volker and Michael D Whinston (2013) "Merger policy with merger choice," *American Economic Review*, Vol. 103, pp. 1006–33.

Nocke, Volker and Stephen Yeaple (2007) "Cross-border mergers and acquisitions vs. greenfield foreign direct investment: The role of firm heterogeneity," *Journal of International Economics*, Vol. 72, pp. 336–365.

——(2008) "An assignment theory of foreign direct investment," *The Review of Economic Studies*, Vol. 75, pp. 529–557.

Norback, Pehr-Johan and Lars Persson (2007) "Investment liberalization: why a restrictive cross-border merger policy can be counterproductive," *Journal of International Economics*, Vol. 72, pp. 366–380.

——(2008) "Globalization and profitability of cross-border mergers and acquisitions," *Economic Theory*, Vol. 35, pp. 241–266.

Ordover, Janusz and Greg Shaffer (2007) "Wholesale access in multi-firm markets: When is it profitable to supply a competitor?" *International Journal of Industrial Organization*, Vol. 25, pp. 1026–1045.

Perry, Martin K and Robert H Porter (1985) "Oligopoly and the incentive for horizontal merger," *The American Economic Review*, Vol. 75, pp. 219–227.

Posner, Richard A (1981) "The economics of privacy," *The American economic review*, Vol. 71, pp. 405–409.

Prat, Andrea and Tommaso M Valletti (2021) "Attention oligopoly," *American Economic Journal: Microeconomics, Forthcoming.*

Prufer, Jens and Christoph Schottmuller (2021) "Competing with big data," *Journal of Industrial Economics, forthcoming.*

Qiu, Larry D and Wen Zhou (2006) "International mergers: Incentives and welfare," *Journal of International Economics*, Vol. 68, pp. 38–58.

Rochet, Jean-Charles and Jean Tirole (2003) "Platform competition in two-sided markets," *Journal of the european economic association*, Vol. 1, pp. 990–1029.

Schweitzer, Heike, Haucap Justus, Kerber Wolfgang, and Welker Robert (2018) *Modernisierung der Missbrauchsaufsicht fur marktmachtige Unternehmen*, Vol. 297: Nomos Verlag.

Shapiro, Carl, Shapiro Carl, Hal R Varian et al. (1998) *Information rules: a strategic guide to the network economy*: Harvard Business Press.

Spulber, Daniel F (2009) "The map of commerce: Internet search, competition, and the circular flow of information," *Journal of Competition Law and Economics*, Vol. 5, pp. 633–682.

Stigler, George J (1980) "An introduction to privacy in economics and politics," *The Journal of Legal Studies*, Vol. 9, pp. 623–644.

Streule Ian and Alessia Marazzo (2017) "Claims for damages due to abuse of dominance rely heavily on identifying the correct counter factual case (Analysys Mason and Lear, 2017)," URL: http://ec.europa.eu/competition/publications/reports/kd0417233enn.pdf.

Tag, Joacim (2009) "Paying to remove advertisements," *Information Economics and Policy*, Vol. 21, pp. 245–252.

Valletti, Tommaso M, Steffen Hoernig, and Pedro P Barros (2002) "Universal service and entry: The role of uniform pricing and coverage constraints," *Journal of Regulatory Economics*, Vol. 21, pp. 169–190.

Varian, Hal R (2021) "Seven deadly sins of tech?" *Information Economics and Policy*, Vol. 54, p. 100893.

Williamson, Oliver E (1968) "Economies as an antitrust defense: The welfare tradeoffs," *The American Economic Review*, Vol. 58, pp. 18–36.

Wilson, Kyle (2021) "Does public competition crowd out private investment? Evidence from municipal provision of internet access," *NET Institute Working Paper, under review.*

Concurrences Review

Concurrences is a print and online quarterly peer reviewed journal dedicated to EU and national competitions laws. It has been launched in 2004 as the flagship of the Institute of Competition Law in order to provide a forum for academics, practitioners and enforcers. Concurrences' influence and expertise has garnered interviews with such figures as Christine Lagarde, Bill Kovacic, Emmanuel Macron and Margrethe Vestager.

CONTENTS

More than 12,000 articles, print and/or online. Quarterly issues provide current coverage with contributions from the EU or national or foreign countries thanks to more than 1,500 authors in Europe and abroad. Approximately 35 % of the contributions are published in English, 65 % in French, as the official language of the General Court of justice of the EU; all contributions have English abstracts.

FORMAT

In order to balance academic contributions with opinions or legal practice notes, Concurrences provides its insight and analysis in a number of formats:

- Forewords: Opinions by leading academics or enforcers
- Interviews: Interviews of antitrust experts
- On-Topics: 4 to 6 short papers on hot issues
- Law & Economics: Short papers written by economists for a legal audience
- Articles: Long academic papers
- Case Summaries: Case commentary on EU and French case law
- Legal Practice: Short papers for in-house counsels
- International: Medium size papers on international policies
- Books Review: Summaries of recent antitrust books
- Articles Review: Summaries of leading articles published in 45 antitrust journals

BOARDS

The Scientific Committee is headed by Laurence Idot, Professor at Panthéon Assas University. The International Committee is headed by Frederic Jenny, OECD Competition Comitteee Chairman. Boards members include Bruno Lasserre, Mario Monti, Howard Shelanski, Richard Whish, Wouter Wils, etc.

ONLINE VERSION

Concurrences website provides all articles published since its inception, in addition to selected articles published online only in the electronic supplement.

WRITE FOR CONCURRENCES

Concurrences welcome spontaneous contributions. Except in rare circumstances, the journal accepts only unpublished articles, whatever the form and nature of the contribution. The Editorial Board checks the form of the proposals, and then submits these to the Scientific Committee. Selection of the papers is conditional to a peer review by at least two members of the Committee. Within a month, the Committee assesses whether the draft article can be published and notifies the author.

e-Competitions Bulletin

CASE LAW DATABASE

e-Competitions is the only online resource that provides consistent coverage of antitrust cases from 55 jurisdictions, organized into a searchable database structure. e-Competitions concentrates on cases summaries taking into account that in the context of a continuing growing number of sources there is a need for factual information, i.e., case law.

- 18,000 case summaries
- 3,000 authors
- 85 countries covered
- 30,000 subscribers

SOPHISTICATED EDITORIAL AND IT ENRICHMENT

e-Competitions is structured as a database. The editors make a sophisticated technical and legal work on all articles by tagging these with key words, drafting abstracts and writing html code to increase Google ranking. There is a team of antitrust lawyers – PhD and judges clerks - and a team of IT experts. e-Competitions makes comparative law possible. Thanks to this expert editorial work, it is possible to search and compare cases by jurisdiction, legal topics or business sectors.

PRESTIGIOUS BOARDS

e-Competitions draws upon highly distinguished editors, all leading experts in national or international antitrust. Advisory Board Members include: Sir Christopher Bellamy, Ioanis Lianos (UCL), Eleanor Fox (NYU), Frédéric Jenny (OECD), Jacqueline Riffault-Silk (Cour de cassation), Wouter Wils (King's College London), etc.

LEADING PARTNERS

- Association of European Competition Law Judges: The AECLJ is a forum for judges of national Courts specializing in antitrust case law. Members timely feed e-Competitions with just released cases.

- Academics partners: Antitrust research centres from leading universities write regularly in e-Competitions: University College London, King's College London, Queen Mary University, etc.

- Law firms: Global law firms and antitrust niche firms write detailed cases summaries specifically for e-Competitions: Allen & Overy, Baker McKenzie, Cleary Gottlieb Steen & Hamilton, Jones Day, Norton Rose Fulbright, Skadden, White & Case, etc.

INSTITUTE of Competition Law
Antitrust databases and resources

The Institute of Competition Law

The Institute of Competition Law is a publishing company, founded in 2004 by Dr. Nicolas Charbit, based in Paris, London and NewYork. The Institute cultivates scholarship and discussion about antitrust issues though publications and conferences. Each publication and event is supervised by editorial boards and scientific or steering committees to ensure independence, objectivity, and academic rigor. Thanks to this management, the Institute has become one of the few think tanks in Europe to have significant influence on antitrust policies.

Aim

The Institute focuses government, business and academic attention on a broad range of subjects which concern competition laws, regulations and related economics.

Boards

To maintain its unique focus, the Institute relies upon highly distinguished editors, all leading experts in national or international antitrust: Bill Kovacic, Mario Monti, Eleanor Fox, Laurence Idot, Frédéric Jenny, Ioannis Lianos, Richard Whish, etc.

Authors

3,800 authors, from 55 jurisdictions.

Partners

- Universities: University College London, King's College London, Queen Mary University, Paris Sorbonne Panthéon-Assas, etc.
- Law firms: Allen & Overy, Cleary Gottlieb Steen & Hamilton, Baker McKenzie, Hogan Lovells, Jones Day, Norton Rose Fulbright, Skadden Arps, White & Case, etc.

Events

Brussels, Hong Kong, London, New York, Paris, Singapore and Washington, DC.

Online version

Concurrences website provides all articles published since its inception.

Publications

The Institute publishes Concurrences Review, a print and online quarterly peer-reviewed journal dedicated to EU and national competitions laws. e-Competitions is a bi-monthly antitrust news bulletin covering 85 countries. The e-Competitions database contains over 18,000 case summaries from 4,000 authors.

www.ingramcontent.com/pod-product-compliance
Lightning Source LLC
Chambersburg PA
CBHW071348230926
51846CB00002B/481
9781954750999